TREATING ANGER, ANXIETY, AND DEPRESSION IN CHILDREN AND ADOLESCENTS

TREATING ANGER, ANXIETY, AND DEPRESSION IN CHILDREN AND ADOLESCENTS

A Cognitive-Behavioral Perspective

Jerry Wilde, Ph.D.

ACCELERATED DEVELOPMENT
A member of the Taylor & Francis Group

USA	Publishing Office:	ACCELERATED DEVELOPMENT
		A member of the Taylor & Francis Group
		1101 Vermont Avenue, N.W., Suite 200
		Washington, DC 20005-3521
		Tel: (202) 289-2174
		Fax: (202) 289-3665
	Distribution Center:	ACCELERATED DEVELOPMENT
		A member of the Taylor & Francis Group
		1900 Frost Road, Suite 101
		Bristol, PA 19007-1598
		Tel: (215) 785-5800
		Fax: (215) 785-5515
UK		Taylor & Francis Ltd.
		4 John Street
		London WC1N 2ET
		Tel: 071 405 2237
		Fax: 071 831 2035

TREATING ANGER, ANXIETY, AND DEPRESSION IN CHILDREN AND ADOLESCENTS: A Cognitive-Behavioral Perspective

1 2 3 4 5 6 7 8 9 0   B R B R   9 8 7 6 5

This book was set in Times Roman by Sandra F. Watts. Technical development and editing by Cynthia Long. Cover design by Michelle Fleitz. Printing and binding by Braun-Brumfield, Inc.

A CIP catalog record for this book is available from the British Library.
∞ The paper in this publication meets the requirements of the ANSI Standard Z39.48-1984 (Permanence of Paper)

Library of Congress Cataloging-in-Publication Data
Wilde, Jerry, date.
    Treating anger, anxiety, and depression in children and adolescents: a cognitive-behavioral perspective/Jerry Wilde.
        p. cm.
    Includes bibliographical references and index.

    1. Rational-emotive psychotherapy.   2. Child psychotherapy.   3. Adolescent psychotherapy.   I. Title.
RJ505.R33W553   1995   95-36561
618.92'8914—dc20   CIP

ISBN 1-56032-481-3 (cloth)
ISBN 1-56032-482-1 (paper)

TABLE OF CONTENTS

PART D ANXIETY

PART E DEPRESSION

PART F GROUP WORK

LIST OF FIGURES

ACKNOWLEDGMENTS

Many individuals have assisted me in the production of this book.

My wife, Polly Wilde, has been tremendously helpful. She also has graciously allowed me to spend many lonely hours necessary for preparing this work.

Through their development and demonstration of counseling skills, my students at Ottawa University have confirmed that this book can be a beneficial addition to clinicians' libraries.

To my colleague Sandy Tellefson . . . your skills and dedication to children never cease to amaze me. Thank you for continually reminding me that the only thing that really matters is the welfare of the kids.

The ideas contained in this book are inspired by the work of Dr. Albert Ellis, who has dedicated his life to helping his fellow man. I hope this book does an adequate job representing his life's work.

This book is dedicated to a 27-year-old male who gave me the greatest gift of all . . . a second chance at life. If it were not for his selfless act of love, you would be doing something other than reading this book. Please support organ donation.

Most of this book was written while listening to Van Morrison. Thanks for the Celtic soul music, Van.

To the readers . . . I know many of you work in desperate conditions and receive a fraction of the support and recognition you deserve. God bless you. Know that your efforts are crucial because you have the most important jobs in the world.

Finally, thanks goes to my daughter, Anna, who has taken me to a level of love and happiness I never thought possible. Daddy loves you very, very much.

PART A
FUNDAMENTALS
OF RATIONAL-EMOTIVE
BEHAVIOR THERAPY

Chapter 1

INTRODUCTION

The need for quality mental health services never has been more apparent. Schools and private practices are flooded with children and adolescents who have serious emotional and behavioral problems. Parents also are searching for sources of support due to the strain these children place upon the family.

In these days of shrinking health care dollars, it can be difficult to secure the resources clients need to receive treatment. Inpatient hospitalization often is limited due to the high cost of such services. When hospitalization is approved, it is often for such a short duration that it has little or no impact on the presenting problem(s).

Extended outpatient psychotherapy also is becoming harder to obtain. Therapists find themselves justifying, arguing, and pleading with managed care representatives who cannot grasp the seriousness of particular cases. The industry's standard of six sessions is not nearly the time needed to bring about significant and lasting change. At the end of the customary six sessions, therapists often are left feeling they have laid the groundwork for growth to occur but are out of time. Therapy is unlikely to continue if the insurance company will not authorize additional sessions. Fewer and fewer parents can afford to pay out of their own pockets for psychotherapy.

News of these shortages apparently has not reached the children! They continue to have emotional and behavioral problems, which should come as no surprise when one considers they live in a culture with a divorce rate approaching 50% as compared to sixteen 16% in 1950. Children from divorced families have been found to suffer from a wide range of emotional difficulties. A 1989 survey of teenagers discharged from a psychiatric hospital found that 84% were living in a disrupted family when they were admitted (Merskey & Swart, 1989). The number of teenagers admitted to private psychiatric hospitals has increased 15-fold since 1971 even though the adolescent population has shrunk over the past 25 years. Does anyone want to wager on the chances of that trend continuing?

Never before in our country have so many children been raised in poverty. The number of children living in poverty has increased from 16% in 1979 to 20% in 1988. America has the dubious distinction of having the highest poverty rate of any industrialized nation. The rates of poverty in Australia and Canada are nearly 15%, but European and Scandinavian countries have less than half the American poverty rate of 20%. There are 2.5 million more children below the poverty level today than in 1980.

Not only are more and more children becoming disturbed, they are becoming disturbed earlier in their lives. Only a few years ago it seemed somewhat unusual to hear stories of grade school children involved in serious crime. Unfortunately, this is no longer true. Incidents such as bomb threats in schools, weapons in lockers, and teachers assaulted in their classrooms are becoming commonplace across the country. Things probably will get worse before they get better, and maybe that is why you bought this book.

The focus of the book will be on the "big three" (i.e., anger, anxiety, and depression). My reasons for addressing these three disorders have to do with my belief that an overwhelming majority of childhood mental health disorders are contained within this trio. For example, *guilt, shame, low self-esteem*, and a *lack of assertiveness* can all be loosely categorized under the heading of *depression* as all result from similar ideas about oneself. Similarly, *phobic reactions, panic attacks*, and *excessive nervousness* are all *anxiety* disorders.

This book presents some basic theoretical information about rational-emotive behavior therapy (REBT) but will focus mainly on specific techniques and case examples. Each of the three disorders will have a chapter devoted to (1) etiology, (2) the best interventions to be used with that particular disorder, (3) ideas and lessons for group counseling, and (4) transcripts from a session or sessions with a client addressing the disorder under examination.

My hope is that you will find the REBT approach useful. While it is focused primarily on solving problems, it is also a "deep therapy" in that REBT frequently affects clients in areas of their lives not being addressed in counseling. It is not uncommon for children to present with a specific problem but also to exhibit sign of significant improvement in other areas as well. REBT is deep enough to bring about a fundamental philosophical change in clients that can have dramatic effects across a wide range of situations.

Once clients have an understanding of the techniques necessary to think and act in a rational manner, they will be able to solve a majority of problems on their own. It is comparable to the old saying, "If you give a man a fish, he eats today. If you teach a man how to fish, he eats tomorrow." REBT teaches children how to fish.

My humble goal is to pass on my understanding of the theory and technique of REBT, allowing readers to teach their clients skills to be used in present-day as well as future situations. Professionals who work with children and adolescents face challenging tasks, but their work is far too important to be unprepared. Their clients' future, and by extension our futures, depend on it.

Chapter 2

THEORY AND DEVELOPMENT OF RATIONAL-EMOTIVE BEHAVIOR THERAPY

The originator of rational-emotive behavior therapy (REBT), Albert Ellis, was born in Pittsburgh, Pennsylvania in 1913. When I asked Ellis if he spent his entire childhood in Pittsburgh he responded, "No, at the age of four I convinced my parents to get me out of that smoky city, so we moved to New York." He has lived there ever since.

During his childhood Ellis had serious illnesses and eventually developed diabetes. Despite his health difficulties, he has lead a productive life and refused to let his ailments slow him down. I recently had the chance to hear him speak again, and at the age of 81, he was still in classic form. Ellis lectured for nearly nine hours on the use of REBT with families, using only a handful of note cards.

At the age of 12 Ellis already had decided he wanted to pursue a career in writing. In order to secure enough money to give him the time and freedom to write, he enrolled in the City College of New York and majored in business administration. The Great Depression of the 1930s made it difficult to prosper in business, so Ellis turned his attention directly to writing and produced numerous manuscripts. While several of these manuscripts received interest from editors, none were published.

Ellis found that he had an interest in the areas of marriage and sex therapy. Ellis seemed to have the ability to advise his friends and family with their personal problems and enjoyed doing so. He decided to become a psychologist and enrolled in the clinical psychology program at Columbia University. Believing that psychoanalysis was the deepest form of therapy, he was trained in the practice by an analyst from the Karen Horney school and began practicing classic psychoanalysis in 1947.

He soon became dissatisfied with classic psychoanalysis as a means of treatment. On several occasions, Ellis has stated that he appears to have been born with a "gene for efficiency," and he abandoned traditional analysis for the following reasons:

1. Psychoanalysis took a considerable length of time. Often patients were in treatment literally for years.
2. One of the cardinal tenets of psychoanalysis is "with insight comes cure." That is, once clients understand the nature of the conflict, they will be able to overcome their difficulties. Ellis (1962) found that even after clients apparently had gained insight into their problems, they continued to act in the same disturbed manner.
3. While some clients improved under psychoanalytic treatment, very few improved substantially.

In the spring of 1955, Ellis began experimenting with new techniques such as having the client sit upright rather than lie on a couch as is the common practice in traditional psychoanalysis. However, many of the problems associated with traditional psychoanalysis also plagued this face-to-face psychoanalysis.

Ellis also began to be more active and directive in his therapy sessions. Rather than waiting for clients to gain insight into the nature of a conflict, Ellis would point out directly the inconsistencies in the client's reasoning. Ellis (1962) commented, "Much to my surprise, this more superficial method actually started to produce not only quicker but apparently deeper and more lasting effects" (p. 8).

In the first outcome study using this new method of psychotherapy, Ellis (1957) compared REBT, orthodox psychoanalysis, and what he referred to as psychoanalytically oriented (PAO) therapy, which was described earlier as face-to-face analysis. Ellis compared 78 cases using REBT with PAO using a sample composed of 61 neurotics and 17 borderline psychotics. Twelve neurotics and four borderline psychotics were treated using orthodox psychoanalysis. The number of treatments using REBT, PAO, and orthodox analysis were 26, 35, and 93, respectively. Ellis rated each case as either little or no progress, some improvement, or considerable improvement. Results were as follows: For orthodox psychoanalysis, 50% exhibited little or no improvement, 37% appeared to have some improvement, and 13% had considerable improvement. For PAO, results were 37%, 45%, and 18%, respectively. With REBT, the results appeared to be superior: 10% had little or no improvement, 46% exhibited some improvement, and 44% had improved considerably.

Ellis initially called this new approach *rational therapy*, but the moniker lead some to believe that the sole emphasis in this new form of therapy was on cognitions (i.e., thoughts and beliefs) (Dryden, 1990). Ellis always had maintained that cognitions, emotions, and behavior are interrelated. He wanted his new form of therapy to emphasize all three components and their interactions. The name was changed in 1961 to *rational-emotive therapy* (RET) to also avoid incorrect associations with the philosophical approach known as rationalism, which RET opposed.

Ellis always maintained that RET could have been called *rational-emotive-behavioral therapy* because RET also encouraged clients to put their new beliefs into practice by acting upon them. In 1993, Ellis once again changed the name, this time to *rational-emotive behavior therapy* (REBT).

Ellis (1985) claimed that he developed the basic principles of his therapy as he worked on overcoming his own anxieties. At the age of 19, Ellis was very shy around women and felt as though his shyness was keeping him from enjoying female companionship. In hopes of overcoming his shyness, he decided he would speak to 100 females at the Bronx Botanical Gardens over a period of one month. Ellis (1992) reported that he actually spoke to more than 100 women. Most quickly left after he approached them. Ellis pointed out that if the doctrines of behaviorism were correct, he quickly would have stopped approaching these women as he was receiving no reinforcement for his labors. He decided to persevere nonetheless and managed to get one woman to agree to meet him for a date, but she never showed up at the time of their scheduled meeting.

While he did not manage to arrange a single successful date, Ellis discovered that he was no longer afraid of being rejected by women. Once he approached women and spoke to them, his anxiety quickly disappeared.

THEORETICAL FOUNDATIONS OF REBT

Ellis has stated that he enjoyed reading philosophers, and the work of certain philosophers had an impact on the development of REBT. Ellis was influenced by the Roman philosopher Epictetus who stated, "Men are disturbed not by things, but by the views they take of them." In other words, *people feel how they think.*

Make note of the fact that this does not proclaim, "People feel as well as others treat them." A common misconception is that other people and events cause emotions. It comes as a shock to many people that others can not *make* them upset (i.e., depressed, anxious, or angry). Most children simply do not believe that being held in from recess, for example, did not make them enraged or that being rejected for a date did not cause their depression. In reality, people upset themselves with their thoughts and evaluations *about* the event.

To illustrate this point, let us take an example in which 10 students are going to take a geometry test. Would all 10 react in the same manner? That is doubtful, as the students would experience a range of emotions. Some would be anxious, some would be indifferent, and some even could be happy. The individual emotional responses would be determined by the thoughts they had concerning the event (taking a geometry test). Once again, people feel how they think.

Students who made themselves anxious would probably be thinking something such as, "This is going to be horrible! I'll probably flunk this test and have to retake the class this summer. My life is ruined." Indifference could be produced by the belief, "Another geometry test. No big deal." A student even could be happy if he/she believed, "I studied a lot for this test and I am ready to take it," or "I am glad there is a test because that way we will not have to listen to the teacher lecture!"

If a particular event caused a specific emotion, how could the same event produce several different emotions for several different people? Logically, it could not, which supports the idea that events do not create emotions. Beliefs or ideas about events determine emotional reactions.

Beliefs can be either *rational* or *irrational* depending on several factors. A belief that promotes survival and happiness generally is considered to be rational. Walen, DiGiuseppe, and Wessler (1980) provided the following information as a guide to determining whether or not a belief is rational:

Rational beliefs
- are true;
- can be supported by evidence or proof;

- are logical;
- are *not* absolute commands;
- are desires, wishes, hopes, and preferences;
- produce moderate emotions such as sadness, irritation, and concern; and/or
- help one reach one's goals.

Irrational beliefs
- are false;
- lead to inaccurate deductions;
- often are overgeneralizations;
- are commands, shoulds, and needs;
- lead to disturbed emotions such as depression, rage, and anxiety; and/or
- hinder one from reaching one's goals.

Irrational beliefs often are produced by overgeneralizations. Ellis (1977a) stated that a *belief remains rational so long as it does not extend an evaluation of the action into an evaluation of the person.* It is best to keep this distinction in mind when working with clients who have emotional problems because many will overgeneralize or exaggerate the significance of an event. Many believe that if someone acted badly, he/she is a bad person. This is a classic example of the type of overgeneralizations that are common in the thinking of children and adolescents, especially those who have emotional difficulties. This type of black or white thinking leads to conflicts due to the fact that we live in a world with many shades of gray. Many children (and adults for that matter) do not understand that there are no bad people, just people who at times act badly.

Maultsby (1975) encouraged clients to ask the following questions to determine if a belief is rational:

1. Can I prove this belief to be true?
2. Does this belief help to protect my life and health?
3. Does this belief help me get what I want?
4. Does this thinking help me avoid unwanted conflicts with others?
5. Does this belief help me feel the emotions I want to feel?

If the answer is "yes" to any three of the above questions about a belief, it is mostly rational. If two or fewer are answered affirmatively, a belief is irrational and self-defeating.

TWELVE IRRATIONAL BELIEFS

Ellis (1977b) detailed 12 major irrational beliefs, which are listed below along with their rational alternatives.

The idea that one must—yes, must—have sincere love and approval all the time from all the people one finds significant instead of the rational idea that no one *has* to have what he/she wants, including love and approval. By turning something that is desirable (such as love and approval) into something that is a necessity, people will be anxious and depressed without the love and approval they believe they must have.

As infants, people are dependent on the love and care of others for survival. This is the only time when a person requires love, and it may be argued that what is needed by an infant is really care and nourishment, which can be provided without love.

No solid evidence exists that a person will perish without love, yet many people will claim that this is a fact. There is support for the idea that a baby will not develop fully without adequate stimulation, but that does not mean the baby will die. Some people hold onto the idea that people need love well past infancy even into adulthood. While it is true that almost all people would like and prefer to have love, no adult needs love to survive.

Love is essentially someone else's opinion of another person. An opinion can be ignored if disagreed with and does not have any *real* power to help or harm anyone. People have the tendency to take other's opinions of them as facts rather than as arbitrary ideas subject to factors outside logical analysis. Some people dislike and hate another person for no reason or for reasons outside the other person's control, such as that person's sexual preference or ethnic background.

Trying to be loved and approved of by everyone is not only unrealistic and unobtainable but will cause individuals to waste a good deal of time and energy (Wilde, 1992). It is wiser for people to concentrate on accepting themselves and their positive (and negative) traits than to be overly concerned with the opinions of others. People cannot control what others think anyway.

The idea that one must prove oneself thoroughly competent, adequate, and achieving, or that one must at least have real competence or talent at something important, rather than the rational idea that *doing* is more important than *doing well*. A common REBT motto is, "Do, don't stew."

Another commonly held overgeneralization occurs when there is confusion between a person's successes or achievements and his/her inherent value as a person. Succeeding does not make an individual worthwhile, and failing does not make an individual worthless.

A belief held by many in this society is that a person's worth somehow can be measured or proven by the level of success he/she obtains in school, athletics, career achievements, or some other area. Many consider that unconditionally accepting a child as worthwhile regardless of his/her behavior or achievement is conceited and wrong. In effect, children are taught that they have to earn their value. An article published in the *Journal of Rational Recovery* (Wilde, 1993a) goes into more detail on this point, stating that it is much more logical to accept an individual as inherently valuable and worthwhile than to equate a person's value with his/her accomplishments. People have no way of proving themselves either valuable or worthless, regardless of their achievements. Children's value and children's achievements are two separate but often confused entities.

The idea that people who do harm or commit misdeeds rate as generally bad, wicked, or villainous individuals who one should severely blame, damn, and punish for their sins rather than the rational idea that all humans are prone to mistakes. REBT reminds us that it is irrational to extend a belief from the behavior to the person. That is, the behavior can be rotten, but the person is not. It is possible for a person to behave in a reprehensible manner but still not be a reprehensible person.

To blame others for one's mistakes is easy, but one needs to remember that all humans are fallible and prone to errors. To expect people to be perfect is a failure to accept reality. Any person would resent others expecting him/her to be mistake free, yet people often do not extend any grace to others and demand perfection.

The fact remains that people have the right to act in any manner they desire, even if others do not understand, appreciate, or agree with their behavior. People acting in selfish and inconsiderate manners have the right to do so given the fact that they are human and possess free will. As such, humans are sometimes prone to use their free will inappropriately.

The idea that life proves awful, terrible, horrible, and catastrophic when things do not go the way one would like them to go rather than the rational idea that many things are inconveniences but there are very few catastrophes other than in the mind.

Words like "terrible," "awful," and "horrible" mean "worse than 100% bad," which is beyond reality. Nothing can be worse than 100% bad. Nothing is so bad that it cannot be withstood. It is, however, certainly possible to exaggerate an event's unfortunate occurrence into an apocalyptic catastrophe, thereby creating unneeded anxiety.

Even death is entirely "standable." When that time eventually comes, as it will for everyone, people will stand death because they have no other choice. Some may not stand it well, but all must stand it due to the lack of other options!

The idea that emotional misery comes from external pressures, and that one has little ability to control feelings or rid oneself of depression and hostility, rather than the rational idea that individuals feel how they think and, therefore, have tremendous control over their reactions, thoughts, and emotions. By believing that others have the power to upset them, people give away their freedom and grant others control.

Nearly any event that could be thought of as fortunate (e.g., winning the lottery) could also produce other feelings (e.g., annoyance at newfound "friends" and relatives who would like to take advantage of newfound wealth). Conversely, almost any event that is viewed as unfortunate (e.g., being fired from a place of employment) could also be thought of in a way to produce different emotions (e.g., now the person who has been fired is free to pursue a new, potentially more rewarding career).

A far too common practice is for people to adopt the role of the victim. People seem to be comfortable in this role, and therefore it has a certain appeal. The idea that people have a great deal of control over their feelings and behaviors does not come as good news to some. While this information is empowering, it can be frightening because it takes away the scapegoats people have been blaming for their difficulties and places responsibility back in their lap.

The idea that if something seems dangerous or fearsome, one must be terribly occupied with and upset about it rather than the rational idea that worrying about an event will not keep the event from occurring. It is appropriate to be "concerned," because concern may help an individual take the appropriate measures to be prepared for a potentially unpleasant event. To be overly concerned is a waste of time and energy and limits a person's ability to enjoy everyday pleasures that may present themselves.

If the feared event does take place, it will be "standable" but perhaps not enjoyable. Many times the imagination of the event is worse than the reality. Most things people worry about never come to pass anyway.

The idea that one will find it easier to avoid facing many of life's difficulties and self-responsibilities than to undertake some form of self-discipline rather than the rational idea that the so-called easy way is invariably much harder in the long run (Trimpey, 1992). Taking shortcuts usually leads to more difficulties in the future. Often the "longcut" turns out to be the best course of action.

Avoiding a problem does not make the problem go away. Eventually the situation will have to be dealt with in one manner or another. Facing a difficult situation head-on may be the best way to deal with the problem. At least the problem will be done with, regardless of the outcome.

The idea that one's past remains all important and that, because something once strongly influenced one's life, it has to keep determining one's feelings and behavior today rather than the rational idea that the past has an influence over the present but does not determine one's actions today. The past does indeed give people "tendencies," but people can become aware of their predispositions and work to make them less of an influential factor in their lives.

The past really does not exist except in memories, and those memories are only impressions of the past as it was then seen. Memories are influenced substantially by individuals' interpretations and selective attention to those events. Many readers undoubtedly have heard the expression that there always are three sides to any story: "(1) his/her side, (2) your side, and (3) what really happened." No such thing as objective history exists, because each individual will create his/her own interpretation of the past.

The idea that people and things should turn out better than they do, and that one has to view problems as awful and horrible if one does not quickly find good solutions to life's hassles, rather than the rational idea that there is absolutely no evidence that anything *should* be different than it actually happens to be. Believing otherwise leads to anger and blaming.

Everything is as it should be now. Simply because some situations are painful or unpleasant does not mean that they should not be. Everything is as it should be now because all the prerequisites for a situation to exist have occurred. For example, *should* there be hunger in the world? That question can be answered by determining the prerequisites for hunger. If the prerequisites have been met, then there should be hunger. The prerequisites of hunger would seem to be the following:

1. more people need food than there is food available to feed them,
2. people must be unable to receive the amount of food they require, and/or
3. people with adequate food must not be concerned enough to do what is necessary to distribute food to the hungry.

If these conditions are in effect, then not only should there be hunger but, logically, there *must* be hunger. I am not making light of the heartbreaking problem of hunger in the world. I merely am trying to point out that it is illogical and irrational to believe that things should not be exactly as they are at this time. Once the prerequisites for an event have transpired, the event must occur. Some situations are without perfect solutions, but this fact is not a catastrophe, just a reality.

The idea that one can achieve happiness by inertia and inaction or by passively and uncommittedly "enjoying oneself" rather than the rational idea that people tend to be happiest when creatively absorbed in some type of enjoyable activity.

Individuals who passively take part in life rarely lead satisfying and rewarding lives. Finding a purpose or a goal to work towards usually fills a person with energy and vitally. A goal or rewarding activity also can be used effectively to help cope with difficult situations—as a means of distracting oneself.

Relaxing and recreating certainly have merit, but a life designed only to satisfy these desires is usually empty and without passion. The key in this equation, as it is in many things in life, is finding the right balance between work and play. Too much or too little of either is usually less than ideal.

The idea that one must have a high degree of order or certainty to feel comfortable rather than the rational idea that very few certainties, if any, exist in the universe. Death and taxes are the two exceptions to this rule of course!

Even without order and certainty, it is still quite possible to be relatively happy most of the time. Many people find themselves capable of tolerating uncertainty by refusing to demand that they receive the certainty they would like. As stated earlier, no one has to have what he/she wants. While it is true there would be advantages to having certainties in some instances, this does not mean certainties must exist. The universe is not run according to individuals' desires.

The idea that one can give oneself a global rating as a human, and that one's general self-worth and self-acceptance depend upon the goodness of one's performance and the degree to which people approve, rather than the rational idea that human beings are far too complex to be given an overall rating. People can not be given a grade or a rating like a movie according to the goodness of their actions.

All humans are a combination of both positive and negative traits. These positive and negative characteristics do not balance each other out. They exist independently and have no influence to enhance or mitigate one another. With this in mind, the best course of action is simply to accept oneself as inherently worthwhile since to prove or disprove a person's worth is impossible.

People are enormously valuable and worthwhile to themselves because they can act in a manner to satisfy their desires. For example, if a person is hungry he/she is the only person who can decide to get something to eat. That, in and of itself, makes people extremely worthwhile to themselves.

PHILOSOPHY OF REBT

REBT theory states that people are basically *hedonistic* in that they attempt to stay alive, seek pleasure, and avoid pain. *Hedonism* often is looked down upon due to the implication that it leads to selfishness. REBT supports *responsible hedonism* because people live in a social world and their self-interests ideally will make the world a better place to live or at least do not infringe on others' pursuits of happiness.

REBT does not support irresponsible behavior that might sacrifice long-term happiness for immediate gratification. To live for today is desirable but not at the expense of tomorrow. REBT encourages the use of the scientific method to gather information and make decisions. Walen et al. (1980) stated that the methods of science appear to be the best methods for learning about ourselves, others, and the world.

The scientific method begins with a hypothesis and proceeds by searching for evidence to support the hypothesis. If evidence can be found supporting a hypothesis or belief, the belief is said to be rational. If no evidence can be found the belief is deemed irrational. While this is a simplistic explanation, it is useful when working with children and adolescents.

Rational beliefs are not valued in and of themselves. The belief is that thinking rationally leads to more enjoyment and less pain in life. Therefore, rational thinking is a means of promoting survival and increasing happiness. REBT therapists encourage clients to put their interests first most of the time and the interests of others a close second. Sacrificing personal desires to meet the wishes of others is not encouraged unless the client wants to sacrifice himself/herself and finds happiness in doing so.

Some have criticized REBT, believing that it teaches clients to be selfish, but an important point to realize is that REBT does not support infringing on the rights of others in order to satisfy personal desires. REBT theory merely states that individuals had better make certain that their desires are met because no one else is responsible for ensuring their happiness and satisfaction. In fact, no one else can make them happy. As stated earlier, all humans are abundantly worthwhile to themselves because no one else has the power to produce feelings of happiness and satisfaction in them.

People tend to be natural philosophers. In the entire animal kingdom, humans are the only species with metacognitive capabilities. That is, *people can think about their thinking.* Our philosophies about ourselves and our world have a major influence on our feelings and behaviors. In turn, our feelings and behaviors can have an influence on our philosophies. This is what Ellis meant when he stated that thoughts, feelings, and behaviors are interrelated.

REBT theory states that the best way of eliminating unnecessary pain and suffering in life is through basic philosophical change. Counselors and therapists can help children change irrational beliefs from absolute demands to preferences, from catastrophes to inconveniences, and from self-denigration to self-acceptance. If children (and adults as well) can learn to make these modifications in their thinking, they will be in a much better position to enjoy life (Wilde, 1992).

Chapter 3

DIFFERENCES BETWEEN REBT AND OTHER APPROACHES

A multitude of therapeutic approaches can be used to help children and adolescents overcome emotional, behavioral, and familial difficulties. The various systems of psychotherapy tallies in the hundreds. To examine all the various treatments is beyond the scope of this book; however, a brief analysis will be offered regarding a few of the most popular schools of counseling.

REBT will be compared and contrasted with several other approaches by answering the following questions:

1. What are the major theoretical underpinnings of these systems of therapy?
2. What are the advantages/disadvantages of REBT when compared with these approaches?
3. What are the similarities and differences between REBT and competing schools of psychotherapy?

PSYCHOANALYSIS

Psychoanalysis was developed by Sigmund Freud during the later part of the nineteenth century and the early part of the twentieth century. Freudian psychoanalysis focuses on the importance of unconscious drives as one of the primary determinants of behavior. According to Freud, people are not ruled by reason but by primal, unconscious, and often repressed urges.

Psychoanalytic doctrine states that individuals become disturbed due to unresolved conflicts that occur during the first few years of life. Many of these conflicts revolve around relationships with parents. Unsuccessful resolution of the Oedipal and Electra complexes are two examples of the types of conflicts that can lead to neurotic behavior.

Freudian theories regarding the nature of emotional disturbance have been disputed by REBT practitioners. Ellis (1962) maintained that individuals behave in a given way primarily due to their thoughts, beliefs and philosophies and not due to the impact of early experiences. Freudian postulates regarding the importance of early experiences in personality development are largely to blame for the widely held belief that the past is *all*-important in determining present-day behavior. While childhood experiences obviously have an influence on personality characteristics, the past does not determine present-day behavior. A more important factor in understanding present behavior is an individual's thinking at this moment, including his/her interpretations regarding past experiences.

If adolescents have relationship problems, the cause is not that they unconsciously are projecting their anger at their mothers or fathers onto all prospective significant others. For example, if children are angry, they are angry because they are demanding something from their environment. They may be demanding that they not be ignored. This anger is a direct result from an irrational belief such as, "I must have what I want, when I want it."

The problem with this type of demanding ("I must have what I want, when I want it") is that children do not control the universe. Insisting on being treated the way he/she would like may have little or no impact on the child's parents, but it will influence the child's feelings. The child may develop an anger problem that could produce numerous other difficulties in his/her interpersonal life in the future.

GESTALT THERAPY

Gestalt therapy was developed by Fritz Perls who, like Ellis, began working as a psychoanalyst before moving away from Freudian doctrines around 1946. Gestalt therapists believe that it is vitally important for a client to gain awareness of what he/she is *doing* and *experiencing*. Much of this awareness is focused on the physical body and the manner in which the body is trying to express emotions. For example, clients may be asked which part of their body they are most aware of and how that part feels. Clients may state they are aware of their legs, which feel tight. The Gestalt therapist may ask the client something such as, "If your legs could speak, what would they say right now?"

This awareness is important because it is only through awareness that clients can gain self-understanding. Clients are encouraged to be responsible for what they are thinking, feeling and doing. They also are challenged to live in the present, as Perls believed a great deal of pathology was the result of unexpressed feelings from the past. The goals of Gestalt therapy, as outlined by Zinker (1978), are as follows:

1. move toward increased awareness of oneself,
2. assume ownership of one's experiences as opposed to making others responsible,
3. develop skills and acquire values that will allow one to satisfy one's needs without violating the rights of others,
4. become more aware of all one's senses, and
5. learn to accept responsibility for all of one's actions.

While it would be hard for anyone to argue with the goals of Gestalt therapy, there are some concerns regarding Gestalt therapy in practice. Perls believed that too much thinking about one's personal experiences caused clients to avoid their feelings. He discouraged clients from thinking about experiences and over looked the role of cognitive processes in emotional matters.

REBT views the analysis of thoughts as extremely important in therapy. It is only through this analysis that clients can learn to challenge their thoughts and replace irrational, destructive thoughts with rational, life enhancing cognitions.

Gestalt therapy is designed to provide an existential encounter for clients. One of the most common procedures used in Gestalt therapy is the empty chair technique. Rather than complaining to the therapist about the poor treatment the client received from his/her mother, the client is asked to visualize his/her mother sitting in the adjacent chair and speak to the mother as if she were in the room.

According to Gestalt therapy, therapists are not to *teach* during therapy, as clients will become more in touch with the answers to their problems through self-discovery. This is one of the oldest fallacies in mental health and has it's roots in nineteenth-century Freudian psychoanalysis. The belief that with aware-ness and self-discovery clients will naturally learn how to live more effectively *rarely* holds true. As Ellis has pointed out, even after insight occurs, clients often continue to act in the same disturbed manner.

Why should therapists not give clients all the information at the therapists' disposal by using suggestions, interpretations, and explanations to help clients in their struggles? By waiting for the client to stumble upon an insight, a great deal of time and energy can be wasted. Also, most if not all school-aged clients lack sufficient life experiences to be able to make mature decisions. Children certainly should have a say in the decisions that affect their lives, but kids can benefit greatly from the counsel of a caring adult. As I always have maintained, children do a lousy job of raising themselves.

BEHAVIOR THERAPY

The name most closely associated with behavior therapy is B. F. Skinner, who expanded the work of an early learning theorist, E. L. Thorndike. Behav-ioral theory states that a person's behavior is the result of the rewards and punishments he/she receives for a given behavior. Skinner believed it would be possible to predict behavior with great accuracy if the stimuli in an individual's environment could be completely controlled.

REBT disagrees with this type of dogmatic behavioral theory that views people as slaves to their environments. Obviously, the rewards and punish-ments a child receives influence the child's behavior, but the child still chooses the emotional and behavioral response. An important point to realize is that very few stimuli are guaranteed to be either reinforcing or punishing. *Whether a stimulus is reinforcing or punishing is determined by the child's view of the stimulus.*

Most teachers would agree that holding a child in from recess is designed to be punishing. But what if the child is being picked on at recess and staying in the classroom would provide a safer place during that time? Under those circumstances, staying in from recess could be reinforcing.

To take the opposite example, most teachers would feel that not having homework is a reward for working hard during the day. According to behav-ioral theory, not having homework should reinforce children to keep up the hard work. What if a child has a special time to complete homework with Mom and Dad, and the child would miss it if there were no work to take home? To this child, not having homework would not be reinforcing and would not increase the likelihood of continued hard work during class.

The preceding are two of many possible examples that could be used to illustrate that very few events are punishing or reinforcing to all students. Perceptions of the event are the most important factors in determining the effect of a stimulus on a child.

Behavior theory would state that a child having a problem with anxiety must have been reinforced for his/her behavior. A student who is very anxious regarding an upcoming test complains that he/she has a stomachache and is allowed to remain home from school. Such a child is being reinforced inadvertently for being anxious, and the behavior has an increased likelihood of occurring in the future.

The behavioral approach deals only with the surface behavior and fails to deal with the *cause* of the anxiety, which is the irrational belief held by the individual. An event, by itself, cannot cause an emotional reaction without accompanying thoughts, beliefs, and evaluations about that event.

A behavioral approach to reducing anxiety would reinforce a child for controlling his/her school anxiety by rewarding the child with extended curfews, special privileges, or other luxuries. Punishment or negative reinforcement would be used when a child refuses to attend school.

While such approaches may work, they are often inefficient because strict behavioral approaches are only concerned with the behavioral manifestations of anxiety and ignore the root of the problem. A much more effective approach is to attack directly the irrational ideas that cause anxiety.

When behavioral approaches are successful, they work because the interventions (i.e., the administration of rewards and punishments) have brought about a change in the client's thinking. When faced with an upcoming test or speech, students who are anxious would think something such as, "I might fail, and that would be the worst thing imaginable. I'd die!" To feel more relaxed when taking a test, students could tell themselves, "No matter what happens with this test, the sun is going to come up tomorrow. I'm not going to die. If I don't do as well as I would have liked, I'll know I tried my best, and that's all I can do." The latter belief would lead to minimal anxiety and increase the likelihood of the student performing effectively.

CLIENT CENTERED THERAPY

A client centered approach, as developed by Carl Rogers, typically focuses on the therapist possessing three attributes that lead to growth in the client.

1. *Genuineness or congruence,* which means the therapist is "real" or not hiding behind any roles.
2. *Unconditional positive regard,* which means the counselor accepts the client and gives him/her the right to have any and all the feelings that he/she experiences.
3. *Accurate empathic understanding,* or the ability to experience the client's internal reality.

By forming a positive relationship with the therapist, clients can begin to value and accept themselves. Through the therapist's support, clients learn to trust their judgments and gain mastery over their difficulties.

While REBT theory agrees that unconditional acceptance of a client is desirable, it does not consider the relationship between the client and the therapist to be all-important. There are counselors who are drawn to the field who have a strong desire to be needed and who undoubtedly foster dependency from clients. Therapists need to ask themselves, "Whose needs am I serving, mine or the client's?"

REBT does not place as much emphasis on the therapist-client relationship for another reason: Clients may learn to value and accept themselves *because* their therapist values them. The idea, "Because my therapist likes me, I am a likable person," is irrational. A therapist's opinion of a client has nothing to do with the client's value as a human being. Such irrational ideas can foster a dependent relationship between the client and therapist that will interfere with the goals of therapy.

With client centered therapy, a child can get a confusing message regarding his/her behavior and inherent value as a person. Often children have difficulty understanding the difference between the way they *act* and the way they *are*. The idea that someone can be displeased with their behavior but still love them can be confusing. They have the right, as fallible human beings, to make mistakes but must learn that there will be real consequences for their choices.

A delicate balance exists between unconditionally accepting a client and being genuine, which not only implies, but also demands, that counselors be honest about their feelings. How can counselors be honest about their feelings when they experience negative feelings towards clients? Rogerian client centered therapists will explain that it is appropriate to accept clients as people even if they engage in unacceptable behavior. Once again, this double message is difficult to get across to children. Adolescents, for the most part, will be able to comprehend this on an intellectual level but still will feel rejected if they are reprimanded for their behavior.

INDIVIDUAL PSYCHOLOGY/ADLERIAN PSYCHOTHERAPY

Alfred Adler was a contemporary of Sigmund Freud but broke away from Freud early in the twentieth century. Adler believed Freudian doctrines regarding human nature were overly deterministic. Adler also believed Freud focused too extensively on biological and instinctual drives.

Ellis (1962) has given credit to Adler as being Ellis' inspiration while he was devising the fundamental principles of REBT. Like Freud, Adler was interested in the past, but he placed more importance in how people *perceived* the past. Adler stressed social influences rather than the Freudian overreliance on sexual influences.

Adler believed that around the age of six, people develop a *life goal* that can be thought of as their purpose in life. Behavior is purposeful in accordance with the goals that have been set.

Adler was a sickly child, which may explain his focus on overcoming feelings of inferiority. He believed that striving to overcome the feeling of inferiority was innate. He also was convinced that people try to be superior in one area to cope with feelings of inadequacy in other areas. An individual with limited intellectual/academic skills may attempt to be superior in athletics. People do this uniquely by developing their own *lifestyle*.

Adler felt that the degree to which people are socially connected largely predicts the happiness and fulfillment they will experience. Many problems, according to Adler, result from lacking a sense of belonging to a group.

The therapeutic goals in Adlerian therapy are to explore *mistaken life goals* and *faulty assumptions,* which in REBT terms would be called *irrational ideas.*

Adler also believed that in order for clients to become healthy, they must increase their social interest.

To help clients accomplish this, counselors often ask clients to recount their early recollections, which gives information regarding clients' perceptions of themselves and what they anticipate from the future. Adlerian theory postulates that clients remember only the early memories that are consistent with their lifestyle.

Counselors also ask clients to discuss their *private logic* or what REBT would call *internal cognitions/self-talk*. Adler believed that the basic ideas people have about themselves are formulated in childhood and carried into adult life. When these assumptions are faulty, clients tend to become discouraged.

Many parallels exist between Adlerian psychotherapy and REBT. Both focus on the determining of the client's perceptions of events as being important in understanding the client. Both focus on a client's faulty assumptions or irrational beliefs as the keys to neurotic behavior. Many of the concepts are similar but simply use different terminology.

Adler was obviously a major influence on Ellis. REBT focuses more specifically on cognitions and places less emphasis on early experiences, but REBT has borrowed heavily from the individual psychology of Alfred Adler.

Perhaps Adler has not received nearly the recognition he deserves, as he historically has been lumped incorrectly in with many other theorists as a "neo-Freudian." Adler's theories and techniques appear to be getting more attention as of late, and it could be that the mental health community is about to take a closer look at Alfred Adler and his work.

THE ABCs OF REBT

REBT uses a system of problem identification, clarification, and resolution known as the ABCs. This system allows clients and therapists to target irrational beliefs and replace them with rational alternatives. This model is helpful because it gives the therapist and client a common frame of reference from which to work. It also can be visual, as most counselors like to diagram the ABCs on paper or a chalkboard. Adding this visual component is beneficial as it incorporates another modality to help in retrieval of the information.

In the ABC system, "A" stands for the *activating event* that occurs immediately before a client becomes upset. The "A" is "the happening" or "situation." A student could be upset because he/she failed a test, was benched on the soccer team, or a host of other occurrences.

An "A" is usually an event or situation of some type but also can be a thought or image. For example, it would be entirely possible for an individual to make himself/herself upset by remembering a situation in the past. In fact, usually it is thoughts of prior events that trigger depressive thinking. Consider a client who was "dumped" by his girlfriend a few weeks ago. He has had virtually no contact with her but continues to think of her. In this case, the "A" would be the memory of a painful event rather than the actual event itself.

The "C" stands for the emotional *consequence* or feeling experienced. An important procedure to try is to get clients to be as specific as possible when labeling their feelings. A client telling a counselor that he/she feels "bad" is not very helpful, as the term bad could be any number of emotions from angry to depressed to guilty. Also clients possibly could feel a combination of emotions at "C." The above client who is no longer with his girlfriend is not only depressed but secondarily angry due to his perceived poor treatment. In such a case, each emotion is caused by a distinctive thought or thoughts.

As has been illustrated, people frequently believe that "A" causes "C" (i.e., getting tuna rather than jelly on a sandwich causes anger), which is an erroneous belief. There is a middle part—"B"—between "A" and "C" that actually causes the emotion.

"B" stands for *belief,* or what an individual tells himself/herself about the activating event at point "A." When searching for the "B," counselors should try to get clients to focus on the thoughts they had *about the "A."* Many will relay unrelated thoughts such as, "My mom made tuna because she didn't have time to go to the store." Encourage clients to focus on their beliefs about the "A" (i.e., "I understand why you got the sandwich but what are you saying to yourself about getting tuna.").

Beliefs generally can be divided into two broad categories: rational beliefs (RB) and irrational beliefs (IB). Two rules are particularly useful in determining whether a belief is rational or irrational: (1) RBs have or are supported by *empirical evidence,* and (2) RBs produce *moderate emotional responses.* IBs are not supported by empirical evidence and typically produce extreme emotional responses.

Another good definition of rational would be *a response that does not use more emotion than is necessary for the situation.* In effect, a rational response is an appropriate response and is not an overreaction to a situation. An example may help clarify this point.

CASE EXAMPLE

A senor in high school, Amy, is depressed because her parents have filed for divorce. Her parents have been having marital difficulties for some time, but Amy had hoped they would be able to work things out. Here is an ABC analysis of Amy's predicament.

Irrational

A—Amy's parents are divorcing.
At point "B," Amy believes the following:

B—"This will screw up my life forever, and I'll never be able to live through this."
At point "C," Amy feels depressed.
C—Depression

Rational

A—Amy's parents are divorcing.
This time Amy tells herself a rational thought at point "B."
B—"I *wish* I didn't have to face this mess, but I don't have a choice. It will be difficult, but eventually I'll be OK. I'm a senior and will be leaving home for college next year so it won't be a hassle for too long."
Such a thought still leads to upset feelings, but rather than being extremely depressed, Amy feels only appropriate emotions such as sadness and irritation.
C—Sadness, Irritation

Some would argue that there is no real difference between depression and sadness. Some might believe any difference strictly would be a matter of semantics. But REBT distinguishes between sadness and depression in that it is definitely appropriate for Amy to feel sad at the failure of her parent's marriage. Believing that her parents' divorce will "screw up my life forever" is making the event worse than it has to be by exaggerating the repercussions of the divorce. This is another way of saying Amy is using more emotion than is necessary for the situation. The question then arises, "How do you tell if the emotional reaction is appropriate or inappropriate?" This is a commonly asked question and rightfully so.

To depend on the labels used by clients is not safe because clients mean different things when they say things like "sad" and "depressed." Some clients who label their feeling "sadness" actually may feel much worse than clients who describe themselves as "depressed."

Ask clients to rate their feelings on a scale from 1 to 100 regarding the event (1 being low emotion and 100 being high). Next ask, "What would be an appropriate level of sadness for people who are going through the divorce of their parents? What number do you think other people would give between 1 and 100?" If Amy answers that she feels at a level of 90 and that an appropriate level would be 40, there is evidence that the client is overreacting to the event. The client has just stated that she is overreacting by the rating she gave these feelings and the intensity of emotions she believed most people would experience. At this point, it is easy to explain to the client, "If you think an appropriate level would be 40 and you feel 90, you're probably not thinking about this in as rational or realistic a manner as you could be. Our job is to get you to feel an appropriate level of (sadness, depression, etc.) rather than making this worse than it has to be."

A slight variation is to ask the client what the average reaction would be if 100 people were asked to rate how badly they would feel if their parents were divorcing. If the client responds that the average of the 100 people would be 60 and the client feels 90, the client is showing the same overreaction only illustrated differently.

Some critics of REBT mistakenly believe that REBT is preaching a Pollyanna approach to problems ("Don't worry, be happy"). Critics seem to believe that REBT simply instructs clients to deny any negative emotions. This is neither the intent nor the result of REBT.

In the above example, Amy would have every right to feel upset regarding her parents' upcoming divorce because there could be some major changes in Amy's life. It would be appropriate to feel upset and concerned, but REBT encourages clients to think rationally about the situation and keep things in the proper perspective.

The recommendation is that counselors diagram the ABCs with nearly every client, especially early in treatment. Eventually, clients can become proficient at performing their own ABC analyses but it takes practice before they reach that point. Once the irrational belief at point "B" is clearly defined, it is time to move onto "D," which stands for *disputation.*

As the word implies, disputation is the point at which the counselor disputes and/or debates with clients about their irrational beliefs at point "B." There are numerous disputation techniques that will be examined later in this book, but a starting point and excellent initial question is, *"Where's the proof for that belief?"*

> **Therapist:** *Amy, here at point "B" you agree that you are saying to yourself, "This will screw up my life forever and I'll never be able to live through this." Is that right?*
>
> **Amy:** *Yes.*
>
> **T:** *So you believe this is so bad that your life is basically over.*
>
> **A:** *Pretty much.*

T: *Remember how we talked about the differences between rational and irrational beliefs?*

A: (nods head in agreement)

T: *Explain what you remember to me.* (Author's Note: Asking the client to explain a concept is a way to assess whether he/she was listening and comprehending. Oftentimes clients will nod their heads and appear to understand but do not clearly understand what just has been explained.)

A: *A rational belief is like a true idea. An irrational belief isn't true. It's not correct.*

T: *What about proof? Can you remember that?*

A: *Oh, yeah. We can prove a rational belief. Like with the diet pill . . . give the pill to 100 people, and if they lose weight, you've proven it works.*

T: *Good. Now let's get back to your belief about your parents getting divorced. Can you prove that your life will be basically over and that you'll never be able to live through this?*

A: *Yes!* (quite emphatically)

T: *OK. Prove it to me.*

A: *I hate it.*

T: *I didn't ask you whether you liked it or not. I know you don't like it and I understand that. I don't think most people would. I asked if you could prove that this will screw up your life forever.*

A: *What do you mean, "Prove it?"*

T: *You have a belief and I want you to show me evidence that your belief is true.*

A: *I can't show you evidence.*

T: *Then is your belief rational or irrational?*

A: *Irrational, I guess.* (Author's Note: At this point, Amy agrees that her belief is irrational, but it does not appear that she really believes that to be true. More disputing had better be done to convince Amy that her idea does not make sense.)

T: *Have you ever known kids whose parents got divorced?*

A: *Yes, Rhonda's parents got divorced two years ago.*

T: *Would you say Rhonda's life is screwed up forever and that she never will be able to be happy again?*

A: *No, she was mad and scared for a while, but she's doing OK now I guess. She decided to live with her mom, and she visits her dad every other weekend.*

T: *So she had some tough times for a while but hasn't died from her parents divorcing.*

A: *Uh-huh.*

T: *Is it possible that you'll pull through like Rhonda did?*

A: *I guess it's possible, but I'm scared of what's going to happen. They're screwing everything up.*

T: *Let's look at that statement for a minute, because it keeps coming up. Are they screwing everything up or just making some things more difficult?*

A: *They're screwing everything up.*

T: *Are they screwing up the price of tea in China?*

A: (laughing) *No.* (Author's Note: The use of humor can be a very effective way of pointing out to clients that they are exaggerating a problem.)

T: *OK, so they're not screwing up everything. And you know what else? They're not screwing up everything in your life either. Can you name a few things that will go on pretty much as usual?*

A: *Pom squad.* (long pause) *School will be pretty much normal; my job won't really be affected.*

T: *Amy, what I'm trying to get you to see is that your belief that their divorce will end your life is really not true and is only making you feel much worse about the whole thing. Can you see that?*

A: *Yeah, but I still feel bad.*

The next step in ABC analysis is to produce a rational belief to replace the irrational belief at point "B." This usually can be done simply by changing a word or two in the irrational belief, thereby making it rational.

Irrational Belief—"This will screw up my life forever,
and I'll never be able to live through this."

This IB can be changed to an RB simply by substituting a few words.

Rational Belief—"This may make some parts of my life more
difficult for a while, but I will be able to live through this."

The final step is "E," which stands for the new *effect* produced by substituting an RB for an IB. If the above stated rational belief was substituted for the irrational belief, it most likely would produce a moderate emotional response. Instead of feeling depressed as Amy felt at point "C," she probably would feel less depressed (sad) or only irritated. There is a big difference between irritation, which is an appropriate response, and depression, which will do nothing to help her survive, reach her goals, or allow her to experience the emotions she wants to experience.

Some may think, "Why doesn't this student have the right to be upset? By taking away her feelings, aren't we depriving her of a defense against her parents' divorce?" The child or adolescent *does* have the right to be angry or depressed because people have the right to think and feel whatever they want. People can walk around believing that the sun rotates around the earth if they like. However, such thinking does nothing to help them cope with the day-to-day hassles they will run into. Amy's belief that her parents' divorce will end her life is simply wrong. That belief will do nothing but cause more depression and upsetting emotions in similar situations in the future. On the other hand, helping her think better about the situation may help her handle other setbacks that lie ahead in the course of her life.

Helping clients be less upset is not taking away a defense. A much better defense is to arm clients with the power to eliminate self-defeating ideas. When kids learn skills so that people and problems no longer can upset them, students truly are empowered. In this day and age, what better defenses could a child or adolescent possess?

Early on in the therapeutic process, clients have a difficult time changing IBs into RBs. The therapist has to provide assistance until clients become proficient at independently challenging and changing beliefs. This can be problematic because many times the counselor is using his/her words to produce rational beliefs rather than having clients use their own words. It is always best to allow children and adolescents to spontaneously produce their own RBs. One of the best techniques to help clients along in this regard is *rational-emotive imagery* (REI).

REI is a technique that has numerous applications and has been proven to be beneficial in helping clients overcome the effects of their irrational beliefs. During this section of the book, REI will be described as a means of allowing clients to produce their own rational counters to irrational thinking.

The therapist starts by telling the client to get as relaxed as possible in his/her chair with both feet on the floor. It usually works best to have the client place their hands in his/her lap. Following is an example of how REI would be used with Amy.

> **T:** *Amy, I want you to listen very closely to what I say. I want you to be aware only of my voice and focus on what I say. Try to block everything else out of your mind for the time being. Close your eyes and take a deep breath. As you breathe out, notice that you are becoming more relaxed. Each time you breath out you are getting more relaxed and more focused on my voice. The only thing you are aware of is my voice. Imagine you are back in your room two nights ago and you are feeling very depressed about your parents' upcoming divorce. See your room in your mind. Picture all the posters on the walls and everything else that is in your room. Now go ahead and let yourself feel like you did that night. Feel all the depression you felt back then. Stay in your room and try to feel just like you felt two nights ago. When you feel that way, wiggle your finger and let me know you're there.* (Author's Note: It is a good idea to look for behavioral signs confirming that the client actually is feeling the prescribed emotion.) *Stay with that feeling. Keep imagining that you are right there in your bedroom.* (Author's Note: Allow the child to stay in this state for

approximately 20 to 40 seconds. Remind him/her to remain mentally in the situation and to remain upset.) *Now I want you to calm yourself down. Stay in the bedroom in your mind but try to calm down. Instead of being upset, try to get calm. Keep working at it until you can calm yourself down. When you can make yourself calm, wiggle your finger again.*

Usually clients can reach a state of relative calm within a short time. The first question to ask is, *"What did you say to yourself to calm yourself down?"* If the client was able to calm down, he/she had to be thinking a rational thought. The only other way to no longer be upset would be to mentally leave the situation (i.e., no longer visualize the bedroom or change the situation in some way). This usually does not happen, but if it does, the counselor may try the exercise over, encouraging the client to keep imagining the scene but working to calm down.

Clients sometimes will ask, "Am I doing this right?" If they are able to calm themselves down, rest assured that they are doing the procedure correctly. Good results follow from correct procedures. If a client can imagine the situation and not be upset, he/she is thinking rationally.

The RBs that clients produce then can be recorded for use in their homework. A typical RB that might have been produced from Amy's scenario would be, "Even if my parents get divorce I still can find some happiness in life," or "I can stand my parents getting a divorce." The real advantage of using this technique is that the RB comes from the child rather than from the counselor. This technique is worth giving a try because it really is this simple and it really does work this well.

PART B
PRETHERAPEUTIC
CONSIDERATIONS

Chapter 5

INCREASING CLIENT MOTIVATION

Up to this point, the fundamental principles of the REBT approach to psychotherapy have been presented. The major irrational ideas that produce neurotic behavior have been analyzed, and the ABC system of problem identification/resolution has been examined. The reader's understanding of these cardinal tenets will be strengthened during latter portions of this book where the concepts will be applied in various scenarios. Before therapy begins, several additional factors require consideration.

A majority of adult clients are in therapy by their own volition. Even when referred by a physician, it is often the client who has requested the referral for counseling. Even in cases where adults are not self-referrals (i.e., court ordered), they still are choosing to attend sessions. Clients occasionally may say, "The court made me come here," which is actually not true. Even court ordered clients can refuse to attend and suffer the consequences.

A larger percentage of children and adolescents, on the other hand, are not self-referrals. A majority of student referrals are from parents, teachers, administrators, or other school personnel. It is quite common for a teacher to approach a counselor or psychologist and say, "Do you have a minute? I've been concerned about Johnny." A parent may call and say, "I need to talk to someone about my kid." The building's assistant principal will comment, "Something is really bothering Sara."

That is not to say students are incapable of referring themselves. Self-referrals are more common in upper grades as a large percentage of early elementary students are not aware of the counselor's role within their school building.

Even when clients come to a counselor for help, a good many of these self-referrals do not feel in any way responsible for the problem they are experiencing. On a therapeutic level, this means the client does not perceive a need for change. These clients are much more difficult than students who admit there is a problem and want to change.

When a referral is initiated by a parent, it is often in conjunction with the child's teachers. Chances are if the student has been having significant behavior problems at school, there also have been problems at home or in the community. This is not always the case, however, because some clients can control their behavior at school and only have difficulties at home and vice versa.

The referring party or parties usually do not understand the nature of psychotherapy and just want relief from the difficulties the client has been causing. The referring party simply wants things to go better. Certain disorders, such as intense phobias, can nearly overwhelm the entire family.

As an intern I was involved with a child who had a germ phobia. The child was convinced that germs were everywhere and they would make him sick. He would sit down for a meal and ask, "Mom, are you sure there are no germs in the potatoes? Are you sure nobody came in after you washed the glasses and got them dirty?" They had to reassure him throughout the day, and the strain the child was creating was getting to the parents.

Depressed children also produce a lot of tension in the family. They are often irritable and difficult to be around. Parents who are aware their child is depressed also can be haunted by the fear of a potential suicide. These parents want relief for themselves as well as their child and are looking to professionals for help.

Most noncounselors are under the mistaken impression that counselors have the power to *fix kids*. The message a counselor undoubtedly will get from the referring party, either blatantly or subtly, is, "Make this child different!" They do not care how, just do it and do it quickly. Our society has become, to quote my brother, "the culture of the microwave."

I recommend taking the time to explain a few facts when the referral is made. Make it a point to ask if the student has expressed an interest in seeking help. This will allow you to explain that unless the student agrees there is a problem, counseling will be a very difficult process. Therapy is hard with motivated clients and even harder with clients who have no desire to change.

Even if the referring party states that the student does not view the situation as his/her problem, it is still advisable to see the client to assess the situation. There are techniques worth trying to convince clients that it might be time to consider changing their outlook and behavior, one of which is discussed here.

OWNING THE PROBLEM

One of the ways to encourage students to commit to changing is to help them examine all the ways in which their difficulties with anger, anxiety, and/ or depression are causing problems in their lives. For example, many students with anger problems already are involved with the school's discipline procedures and also may have contact with the juvenile authorities. Try to make the association between their difficulties and their temper.

> **Therapist:** *Let me ask you something. Why do you think you and your parents aren't getting along?*
>
> **Chuck:** *I don't know, but they're on my case 24-7* (24 hours a day, 7 days a week).
>
> **T:** *What usually happens? You walk in and they just jump all over you or what?*
>
> **C:** *They start bugging me about school.*
>
> **T:** *Because school hasn't been going too well?*
>
> **C:** *Yeah.*
>
> **T:** *And you do what?*
>
> **C:** *I get pissed off and tell them to mind their own business.*
>
> **T:** *Oh, I see. You get angry because they ask you about school and tell them off or something.*
>
> **C:** *I'm so sick of hearing it.*

> **T:** *Let me take a wild guess here. You get angry and they get angry and yell back.*
>
> **C:** *That's why I don't spend any more time there than I have to.*
>
> **T:** *Do you think you'd yell at your folks if you didn't get angry? If I could teach you a way not to get so mad, do you think things might be a little calmer at your house?*
>
> **C:** *Probably because I wouldn't just yell at them for no reason.*
>
> **T:** *I think you're probably right. The problems start when you get angry and start making some poor decisions. We do some pretty stupid stuff when we get angry, don't we? Or at least I do.*
>
> **G:** *Yeah. I do, too.*

At this point there is at least a window of opportunity provided by the client to explore the problem. The first step (i.e. getting the client to take responsibility for the problem) may have been accomplished, but there is a second hurdle to be cleared.

WILLINGNESS TO WORK

Even if clients readily admit there is a significant problem *they must be willing to work hard practicing the skills they learn between sessions if significant change is going to occur.* Change will not be easy. Altering established behavior patterns is almost never easy. In fact, it is one of the most difficult endeavors to face. Human beings are creatures of habit, and once a routine is established, psychological and biological factors keep these patterns recurring.

Psychologically, the irrational beliefs that produce troublesome emotions often occur at a level below a client's awareness and often go unnoticed. Ask clients, "What were you thinking right before you made yourself feel really uptight?" and a common response is, "I wasn't thinking anything." Inexperienced counselors may take this response as a form of malingering or resistance, but most often clients are being honest. They aren't aware of the thoughts that preceded their anxiety. These cognitions occur almost automatically, and early in therapy clients are not aware of these beliefs.

Biologically, once a habit is established, the neuronal pathways associated with that habit are strengthened each time the thought or behavior is carried out. The dendritic connections operate with increased efficiency, and it becomes increasingly difficult to reroute these pathways the longer the pattern has occurred.

People have the mistaken impression that therapy consists of talking to a counselor once a week and the problem goes away. Actually, it usually takes a lot of practice to learn to handle situations differently, just like anything else in life. An important procedure is to impress upon your clients that if they want to improve at anything, they need to practice.

If someone wants to become a better singer, for example, the only way to achieve that goal is to practice. A person could spend all day thinking about how much he/she wants to be a better singer, but unless he/she actually practices singing, he/she will not improve. The same is true with learning how to control temper or deal with anxiety. People can want to improve with all their heart, but wanting alone will not make it happen.

Another analogy of the process is that of a coach and an athlete. The coach can tell an athlete how to train and what to do in competitions, but the athlete is the one who has to do the training. The greatest coach in the world can not help an athlete who will not train—it is a waste of time for both the coach and the athlete.

ASSESSING MOTIVATION

A practice that I use to assess a client's willingness to work and practice involves a cassette tape and worksheet. I developed the tape, which is about 20 minutes in length and contains basic information regarding REBT, as a way of reinforcing some of the REBT concepts that usually are presented in the first session. The tape and worksheet are especially beneficial in assessing client motivation.

The client is given the tape and instructed to listen to the tape and answer the questions on the worksheet before the next session. The questions on the worksheet are simple, and most clients can answer them without too much difficulty. The tape and worksheet actually are used to determine who is going to spend the time necessary to complete homework assignments. If the client has not completed the worksheet by the next session, he/she probably is not motivated and willing to practice.

If the second session comes and the client has not listened to the tape, I use the opportunity to reemphasize the importance of practicing. If the client will not take the time to listen to a short tape, it is unlikely that he/she will have the self-discipline to do the hard work it will take to learn new ways of handling problematic situations. Of course, clients usually have numerous reasons why they did not get a chance to listen to the tape--they left it at school in their locker, their tape player is not working, or they had a really busy week. I'm not making light of the kinds of excuses kids make, because I hear the same types of excuses from adults.

The best overall predictor of future behavior is past behavior. If clients have a history of being irresponsible, the best bet is that they will continue operating in that fashion in the future. People can and do change but not without considerable effort.

School counselors, psychologists, and social workers have many more potential clients than they have time to serve. Use the tape and worksheet, or some device, to determine which potential clients are ready to work and which are not. That is not to say that a client who is not ready to work will not be motivated at a later date. As mental health professionals, we had better place a high priority on maximizing our effectiveness since there are many children who need help.

People will experience a lot of discomfort before they are ready to change, because the only way some people learn is through pain. Their discomfort can serve them well, however, because through their pain they can become motivated learners. Kahlil Gibran (1923) wrote, *"Your pain is the breaking of the shell that encloses your understanding."* Pain is sent not to punish but to help people understand that it is time to change. It is true that many go through a lot of unnecessary pain before they come to this understanding.

Chapter 6

DISTINCTIONS BETWEEN CHILD AND ADOLESCENT THERAPY

Children and adolescents are similar in many respects but quite different in others. These differences will need to be kept in mind when planning interventions to be used during the course of therapy.

REBT has been criticized by some as only being effective with brighter children. Others mistakenly have stated that REBT can not be used effectively with elementary students. While these assertions are definitely false, it is true that the cognitive limitations of clients had better be taken into consideration.

The most important distinction between children and adolescents (with regards to psychotherapy) is their capacity for abstract thought. If students are not abstract thinkers, then to rely upon interventions that utilize abstract principles as a means of disputing and changing irrational beliefs would be unwise. Most 7-year-olds would be hopelessly confused if a counselor explained to them that it is irrational to say a parent *should not* have grounded them. These concrete thinkers would be unable to grasp the concept that *everything is as it should be now*. In reality, their parents *should* have acted exactly the way they acted simply because that is how they did act.

These same 7-year-olds probably could understand that it would be better to *wish* that they would not have been grounded. They could grasp the notion that to demand they not be grounded is silly because grown-ups make the rules, not the kids.

Adolescents bring about a different set of circumstances and concerns. They can be difficult to understand because they are paradoxical in many regards. Consider the following examples of the apparent contradictory nature of adolescents.

1. Adolescents tend to be egocentric or inner focused and believe that the world has to be as they want it to be regardless of the reality of the situation. Many have not had sufficient life experience to understand or appreciate perspectives different from their own. Anything or anyone who has different ideas is perceived as wrong and as a potential threat.
2. Adolescents tend to be unsure of their skills and abilities but try desperately to hide these insecurities. Some use denial as their defense mechanism of choice, but projecting their weaknesses onto others is also quite common.
3. Teenagers are overly sensitive and have their feelings hurt easily due to their inner focus. The slightest look or wrong word can have a devastating effect on their feelings regarding themselves. On the other hand, a small gesture on the part of someone they look up to can be very beneficial.
4. Since they do not have a clear sense of who they are, they tend to define themselves through their group affiliations or according to how others view them. All humans tend to be gregarious, but this tendency is even more pronounced in adolescence.
5. Teenagers tend to experience mood swings and will go from elation to depression in a matter of minutes. To predict why this happens or when it will occur is difficult.
6. They constantly worry about being too much like everyone else, so they strive for their own look and identity. Conversely, they dislike being singled out or being too different. They have a very thin "comfort zone" in this regard.
7. They are embarrassed by their parents yet depend heavily upon them. They dislike the fact that their parents know them so well and are aware of all their weaknesses and insecurities.
8. A large percentage of teenagers have social anxiety and find it easier to withdraw from social contact even though by doing so they may be missing enjoyable activities. Even when they are isolated they tend to act as if they were performing for an imaginary audience.
9. Adolescents tend to overidealize and spend a lot of time and energy

thinking about "what should be" rather than "what is." As such, they have unrealistic expectations of themselves, others, and the world in general (Wilde, 1992).

WORKING WITH YOUNGER CLIENTS

While some recommendations already have been made for working with younger clients, a few additional suggestions now are offered. The starting point is developing a trusting relationship.

While REBT does not view the relationship with the client as all-important, it does view the relationship as a key component in the therapeutic process. Sincere attempts had better be made to gain the client's confidence. It is virtually impossible to reach a positive outcome without at least a modicum of trust.

REBT holds that having a client's respect is much more important than having his/her admiration. As a colleague of mine, Dr. George Harper, used to say, "That 'liking' stuff just gets in the way of what we're trying to accomplish." It is helpful if clients believe the counselor genuinely wants to help them and has the ability to do so.

One of the most common mistakes is staring continuously at children during the initial session. Forget the ideas taught in graduate school that maintaining good eye contact is a way of showing clients you have a real interest in what they are saying. Too much eye contact will cause many children to feel anxious and self-conscious, which will interfere with their ability to concentrate. Children easily can feel intimidated by adults. Many clients undoubtedly will have low self-esteem to begin with, and the stare of an adult will not set them at ease.

It is best to observe the child in short segments. This allows the child to examine the counselor and the surroundings.

With noticeably anxious children, it can be beneficial to allow them to perform some type of physical activity such as drawing or coloring. The use of art therapy has two advantages: (1) Not only does it allow children to perform some physical activity to help them relax, but (2) it also can be used as a rich source of information. The interpretation of children's drawing can provide insight into the nature of the problem.

It is not advisable for counselors to adopt a "little person's" voice when working with younger children if this is not something counselors would do naturally. Children will sense there is something artificial about such a practice and feel uneasy. To fool some adults might be possible, but to fool children is extremely difficult if not impossible.

This does not mean a counselor should not become more childlike. Something I use with almost all my clients is a secret handshake called "the fist." When time is up for a session, I put out my hand and we touch fists like professional athletes. This is also a good way to let the client know that time is up and the session is over. Kids really enjoy things like special greetings, and these simple procedures bring about a sense of trust. Almost everyone loves secrets, and secrets only are shared between people who trust.

Lastly, one should be oneself. That may mean a counselor will ignore a majority of these recommendations, which is fine if he/she already is establishing good rapport with clients. If building relationships with younger clients is an area in which the reader could improve, he/she might try some of these recommendations. What works for one counselor may not work for another, but the reader can rest assured that these methods are "field tested."

PART C
ANGER

Chapter 7

ANGER

As has been stated previously, most children and adolescents believe that situations outside their control create their emotions. This statement applies to any and all emotional reactions including anger. Clients typically blame their anger on either the actions of others or events they dislike.

Not a day passes without hearing numerous remarks that support the contention that others have the power to make people angry.

- "She made me so mad."
- "If he says that to me, I'll have no choice but to tell him off."
- "When people say things behind my back, I get ticked."

Some of the more popular theories regarding the source of anger state that anger is an emotion *caused* by frustration (Dollard, Doob, Miller, Mowrer, & Sears, 1939). This belief, which has been called the *frustration-aggression hypothesis*, states that when people are frustrated, the aggressive drive is aroused naturally and automatically. The only way this aggressive drive can be reduced is by acting out in an aggressive manner.

According to REBT theory, anger is not being caused by frustration but by the demand that we not be frustrated. Which is correct?

If the frustration-aggression hypothesis were correct, every time a student is frustrated he/she will become angry because frustration *causes* anger. The question then becomes, "Can students experience a negative event such as unfair treatment and not anger themselves?" While nearly all students would dislike being treated unfairly, it is entirely possible that a student could receive such unfortunate treatment and not become overly upset. Students can and do react differently to the same situation.

A student could have received time in detention because he/she was accused of cheating on a test even though he/she actually had not cheated but inadvertently looked across at another student's paper. Instead of thinking and stating, "I didn't cheat. I was thinking, and my eyes were just pointed in that direction. It's not fair!" a child could think, "I knew the rule Mr. Douglas has about keeping your eyes on your own paper. While I didn't cheat, I did make a mistake. Hopefully, I won't be this unlucky in the future." By accepting responsibility for their behavior, children can acknowledge that they had acted inappropriately in some manner and deserved a consequence.

It also would be possible for children to believe that they had been treated unfairly but still refuse to make themselves angry. They could believe, "It's not fair. I really don't deserve this punishment. Mr. Douglas made a mistake, which we all do from time to time. I would like it if I wasn't being treated unfairly, but that's the way it goes sometimes. I can certainly see how he would think I was cheating."

Students still would be disappointed about being assigned to detention but would not be enraged. The rational thought, "It's not fair, but people have the right to make mistakes," would keep the emotional response at an appropriate level.

Ellis (1973) drew a distinction between

1. healthy anger—which is moderate in intensity and includes such feelings as *irritation, disappointment,* and *displeasure* and
2. unhealthy anger—which includes feelings such as *rage, hate,* and *bitterness.* These emotions are deemed unhealthy because they do little to aid in survival and help clients reach their goals. If the child's goal is to be able to avoid detention, rage and hate toward his teachers only will interfere with this goal. Such emotions certainly will not help the child control his/her behavior.

Emotions such as irritation and disappointment are viewed as healthy because they motivate clients to change. Students in the above example who are irritated over receiving detention will try to make certain their eyes do not move accidentally onto another's paper. Irritation or disappointment will do nothing to interfere with their behaving in a manner that will allow them to be included in class activities and will serve as a reminder to follow the class rules.

A common misconception is that REBT does not support an individual's right to be angry. This is patently false as people have the right to feel whatever emotion they are feeling. There are times when it is entirely appropriate to feel irritated and annoyed at someone's obnoxious behavior. In fact, it would be difficult not to be irritated with some situations. This healthy anger is rational.

However, when the feelings reach extremes such as rage, clients no longer are thinking rationally because these emotional extremes are almost always self-defeating. Also, rage and extreme anger usually are produced by thoughts pertaining to the *character of the person,* rather than the *behavior in question.* For example, if someone lies to you, it is rational to feel irritated with the person's behavior but irrational to think the individual is a "rotten person" who should be punished for being such a liar. As long as the evaluation remains focused on the person's behavior, it may be rational. When it extends to the person's character, it is irrational.

Social psychologists have long known of a phenomenon called *fundamental attribution error*, which can be defined as the tendency to attribute others' failings to their dispositions (or characters). Conversely, people attribute their own difficulties largely to situational factors beyond their control. In short, people have the tendency to make excuses for their own difficulties and blame others for their problems and shortcomings.

REBT therapists are not "emotional fascists" who tell clients what they can and cannot feel. People have the right to feel whatever emotions they choose to experience, including rage and hate. Continually feeling such extreme emotions is not advisable because these emotions rarely, if ever, lead to positive results. Extreme emotions such as rage and hate often lead to behavior that is out of control.

Clients often convince themselves and others that events cause them to be angry but, logically, this can be disproved. Events have an influence over the children's emotional reactions and contribute to feelings but are not solely responsible for emotions. This is an important distinction because it is the key to helping children control their anger. It is children's beliefs, attitudes, and ideas about events that are primarily responsible for their emotional reactions.

PRIMARY BELIEF LEADING TO ANGER

Anger is created by a *demand* of some type. Typically the demand is formulated by key words such as *should, must, ought to, have to*, etc.

- The world *should* be fair.
- I *must* have things go my way.
- I *ought* to be able to do what I want.
- I *have* to have respect.

Ellis (1976) stated on numerous occasions that humans have a tendency to escalate their desires or wishes into absolute demands. This is especially true when these desires are strong. The fact that nearly all humans share this habit lead Ellis to believe that this tendency is innate. Undoubtedly this tendency also is influenced by sociocultural factors.

A child may see a candy bar in a store and think to himself/herself, "I really want that candy bar." Is this a rational belief? Absolutely. The child is expressing a desire, and there is evidence to support his/her belief. The fact that the child continually asks his/her parents to buy the candy bar is evidence that the child does indeed want it. The problem lies in the fact that there is typically a second portion to this statement that is an automatic thought and often goes unheard. The second portion adds, "I really want that candy bar, *and therefore I have to have it!*" This second portion is an absolute demand and is the cause of the child's anger.

If the belief were stopped after, "I really want that candy bar," chances are the child might be disappointed without the treat, which is understandable. Possessing the candy bar has significant advantages: (1) If the child is hungry, the candy bar will satisfy the desire for food; and (2) We all know the real advantage of the candy bar is that it tastes good, certainly better than the dinner the child will be served later that evening.

When the second portion of the belief (". . . and therefore I have to have it!") is added and the demand is not met, anger naturally will follow. Trust the REBT conceptualization of anger: If there is anger, there is a demand. Even if clients claim that they are not demanding that the world treat them differently, if anger is exhibited rest assured that a demand is also present.

While the primary beliefs leading to anger are demands in one form or another, secondary corollaries also contribute to anger. These beliefs are considered secondary because they tend to be focused on the nature of the offending party or the nature of the perceived misdeed. Ellis (1977a) stated that the following beliefs (secondary corollaries) also lead to anger:

1. How *awful* for you to have treated me so unfairly!
2. I *can't stand* you treating me in such a manner!
3. Because you have acted in that manner towards me, I find you a *rotten person.*

The term "awful" is an immeasurable and indefinable term. When children and adolescents use the term "awful" to describe an event, they mean "bad" or "very bad." The actual emotional meaning associated with the term "awful" seems to mean "worse than 100% bad," which is impossible. No matter how bad an event happens to be, it could always be worse.

A good technique for helping clients realize that nothing is worse than 100% bad is to have them name the worst event they can imagine. After they have stated their personal "worst event," challenge them to see if they somehow can make the event even worse, which probably will be fairly easy. Most events they will offer are certainly not tragedies in the true sense of the word.

The second corollary that states that an individual "can't stand" being treated in such a manner is irrational because nothing is so bad that it can not be stood. This type of thinking is also an example of exaggerating an event's "badness."

Clients might believe that they cannot stand being treated unfairly when in reality they have been treated unfairly hundreds of times in the past and stood it. To be unable to stand something literally means that if the event were to occur, it would kill the individual. No one ever died as a result of unfairness alone.

The third corollary ("I find you a rotten person.") makes the mistake of overgeneralizing from the evaluation of an act to the evaluation of the person committing the act. No matter how rottenly a person acted, there still are no "rotten people." For someone to be a rotten person would mean that every act the person has committed (or will commit) has been rotten, which is also impossible.

In the simplest of terms, anger is produced by the grandiose belief that "my desires and wishes *must* be fulfilled" (Hauck, 1980). An angry client is taking his/her personal preferences and making these wishes laws. When someone is angry he/she is declaring commandments for the entire universe and then damning people who dare disobey these commandments. The problem with this type of thinking is that no one (including the client) runs the universe.

DIRECTIONS OF ANGER

We have examined the core irrational belief leading to anger (i.e., "Things must/ought/should be as I would like them to be.") This belief produces anger that can be directed at any number of circumstances. Anger typically is projected at one of three individuals or situations:

1. anger at self,
2. anger at others, and/or
3. anger at the world.

Anger at Self

Kids can become angry at themselves in much the same manner that they become angry at anyone or anything. The difference is that instead of another person breaking a universal commandment, it is they themselves who have broken their own personal commandment. Anger at oneself also can lead to depression and feelings of guilt. Clients believe (1) that they have acted as they should not have and (2) that they are "no good/rotten" for doing so. Some students who are perfectionistic have a tendency to become very angry with themselves. They set unrealistically high expectations for themselves, and when they cannot live up to their own expectations, they are angry at themselves.

Sean, a 7th-grader, was a very high achiever both athletically and academically. He was a child who was well-liked by his peers and from all appearances had things under control. A teacher of Sean's explained that he had a hard time accepting criticism, and this became very evident the day the class was going over a test from the previous week. Sean was very angry because he believed that he was not given full credit for some of his answers. He would not accept the teacher's reasons for taking points off, and he became disrespectful toward the teacher.

What appeared to be a child who was angry at his teacher was actually a child angry with himself due to his poor performance on the test. He was projecting the anger onto the teacher, but after he calmed down, he was able to explain to me that he felt that he *should* have done better because he knew the answers. The core irrational belief that Sean possessed was, "I should always be at my very best, no matter what." Sean's irrational thought was uncovered as I developed a logical hypothesis based upon work with other perfectionistic students.

Anger at Others

It probably comes as no surprise that children and adolescents, just like adults, find it easy to make themselves angry at others. REBT therapists (Dryden, 1990; Ellis, 1977a; Grieger, 1982) have pointed out that anger at others typically revolves around four themes. Anger occurs when people (1) are blocked from achieving their goals; (2) are attacked or have their values attacked; (3) are threatened clients or have their values threatened; and (4) have their rules broken by other people.

Anger at the World

A certain percentage of students will be angry with nearly everyone and everything because these people or things are not the way the students would like them to be. These clients are the most challenging. They often learn these irrational beliefs from their parents who also demonstrate this form of *low frustration tolerance.*

While clients have some control over their world, the amount of control is often insufficient to bring about any significant changes in their environments. If it is possible for the client to change some of his/her unpleasant circumstances, he/she should be encouraged to do so. If change is not likely, the client would be best helped by learning to accept the situation and trying to find as much happiness as possible.

Chapter **8**

DISPUTATIONS
AND INTERVENTIONS
WITH ANGER PROBLEMS

Three chapters will be devoted to disputations and interventions recommended for use with anger (Chapter 8), anxiety (Chapter 11), and depression (Chapter 14) problems. Some problems will be unique to anger, anxiety, or depression in particular and will not be mentioned again in the other two chapters. Many problems are presented with all three emotions and will be repeated (with the appropriate variations) in each or the three disputation chapters. Each disputation will have an example of how the intervention is to be applied to the treatment of anger, anxiety, or depression.

REBT uses cognitive, behavioral, and emotive techniques to help clients examine their thoughts and find the errors in their thinking. Thoughts, behaviors, and feelings are continually interacting and influencing one another simultaneously. For example, a thought ("Mrs. Smith isn't being fair") leads a child to behave in a certain manner (withdraw from classroom discussion), and the behavior impacts the emotions the child feels (bored). In reverse, a feeling (anger) influences how a child acts (hits another student), and the behavior affects his/her thoughts ("Billy had it coming for telling on me"). Thoughts, feelings, and behaviors interact simultaneously; therefore, it is helpful to have an arsenal of cognitive, behavioral, and emotive techniques to be used in the disputation process.

Disputations are essential in the practice of REBT because it is through the disputation process that clients are helped to realize that they have been thinking and acting in a self-defeating manner. Having as many disputations as possible is important because some arguments work well with some clients and not as well with others. If the counselor is viewed as a carpenter, these disputations are his/her tools. The more tools one has and the more talented one is at using those tools, the better one will be at one's craft.

COGNITIVE TECHNIQUES

Cognitive techniques encourage rational analysis of a belief to determine whether or not the idea makes sense. "Why" questions can be used effectively in this pursuit.

Louis: *She has no right to tell the teacher I cheated on that test!*

Therapist: *Why not?*

L: *She just can't.*

T: *Why?*

L: *It's not very nice.*

T: *Why can't she act that way though? Why can't she be "not nice"?*

L: *Because I don't like it.*

T: *But why do you have to like the way she acted?*

One of the hardest things for clients with anger problems to accept is that *people have the right to be wrong*. Most individuals are reared to believe that because a majority would find certain acts inconsiderate and inappropriate, humans *must not* engage in those behaviors. It would be nice if people did not act selfishly, dishonestly, or in a rude manner, but that does not mean that they must not.

Another excellent cognitive disputation involves helping clients see that by getting angry at someone, they are giving control to this person. Since the individual they are angered at already has carried out a misdeed against them, it is doubly foolish to let this person control how they feel. By getting angry, clients are letting their agitator win again.

This disputation is a way of letting clients use their anger in a constructive manner. Because they are already upset with the offending party, the therapist can use their dislike of the other person's behavior to motivate them to control their anger.

> **Therapist:** *So let me see if I understand. Mike borrowed your skateboard without permission and you're mad at him?*
>
> **Dan:** *Yeah.*
>
> **T:** *Wow, Mike is getting to win twice.*
>
> **D:** *What do you mean "win twice"?*
>
> **T:** *Well, not only did he get to ride your skateboard all day, but now he's controlling how you feel. He's winning twice.*
>
> **D:** *I've never thought of it that way.*
>
> **T:** *If I were you, I wouldn't want Mike to be able to control how I feel. He already got to show off on your new rig; now he's ruining your day.*

Use of Humor

The use of humor and exaggeration can be used to show clients that they are thinking in an irrational manner and creating their own anger. Humor also can be used to help establish rapport and "lighten" things when need be. Sometimes clients get frustrated with the disputation process and even get angry at the therapist.

> **Therapist:** *So you believe that Mrs. Smith has no right to give you algebra homework on the night of a soccer game.*
>
> **Mitch:** *I don't think that's too much to ask.*
>
> **T:** *Why not also demand that she let you look over the exams in advance? And why shouldn't you be able to take out any questions*

> *you don't like? How about letting you just write the entire exam? And grade it too?*

By exaggerating the situation to a ridiculous extreme, it is hoped that the client will see that it is unwise to demand anything that he/she does not have control over.

Search for Control Technique

As was stated earlier, when students become angry, they are giving away their control, which they do not like to admit. Many clients think that when they are getting angry they are demonstrating power, but in actuality, they are exhibiting weakness. There are a couple of ways of demonstrating this weakness that can be effective.

When clients state, "She made me so mad," try looking around on the floor as if you had lost something. When they ask what you are looking for say, "Your control."

Steve: *Are you looking for something?*

Therapist: *Yes, your control.*

S: *My control?*

T: *Somehow you've lost your control over your feelings. We all have the ability to control how we feel, but somehow you've lost yours. How else could someone make you angry?*

The same technique can be used with students who blame their difficulties on their "bad temper." It is not uncommon for students to blame their temper as an excuse so that they do not have to accept responsibility for their behavior. Students say things like, "I've had a bad temper all my life," or "I've got a bad temper just like everyone in my family."

Melissa: *Are you looking for something?*

Therapist: *Yes, my temper.*

M: *Your temper?*

T: *I lost it about the time I stopped demanding that the world treat me fairly.*

Paradoxical Intention

Paradoxical intention also can be used with clients who have anger problems. For example, if a student is extremely angry at another student, try to convince the client to act especially nice towards his/her agitator, and the client may feel less angry. Also, behaving in this paradoxical manner could encourage the offending party to examine his/her behavior and act more appropriately in the future.

BEHAVIORAL TECHNIQUES

Reinforcement

Reinforcement can be used in a number of different ways during the course of therapy. For example, clients can receive rewards from their parents after homework completion. Some type of behavioral contract can be arranged regarding what reinforcement can be earned for completing the agreed upon assignment. This type of program has the advantage of keeping the parents involved and aware of the client's progress.

Reinforcement also can be used as a means of encouraging clients to stay in control of their behavior. The above mentioned contract can include a section specifying the rewards a client can earn if he/she does not act aggressively. It is important to be behavioral specific in terms of what constitutes "acting aggressively." Parents and the client can work out an agreement with which both sides can live, but it is wise to allow the counselor to have input on the contract.

Rubber Band Technique

A technique that is similar to cognitive distraction but is more behavioral oriented is the rubber band technique. Clients are to wear rubber bands around their wrists. When they feel themselves becoming angry, they are to snap themselves with the rubber band. The snapping of the rubber band is a reminder to practice their rational beliefs immediately.

This technique also can be used when clients hear themselves thinking "shoulds," "musts," "have to's," and "ought to's." When they identify such commandments, they are to snap themselves and replace these irrational beliefs with rational thoughts.

The snapping is a mildly aversive stimulus, but this technique is not a punishment. The snapping is more helpful as a reminder to use rational coping statements.

EMOTIVE TECHNIQUES

Rational Emotive Imagery

Rational emotive imagery (REI) has been examined previously (Chapter 4) and will be only reviewed at this time. REI can be tremendously effective and is my personal disputation of choice with angry clients.

The counselor starts by having the clients picture the scenario where they anger themselves. The counselor encourages clients to become angry but, after a few moments of being upset, calm themselves down. Clients are to continue to imagine the scene but attempt to be only irritated and not enraged.

Forceful Dialogue

As was explained earlier, clients are encouraged to argue forcefully with themselves regarding their irrational beliefs leading to anger.

Irrational: *Teachers have to treat me fairly.*

Rational: *It would be nice if teachers treated me fairly, but there isn't any evidence that they have to do so.*

Irrational: *But they should be fair.*

Rational: *There is not one reason why they should act any other way than the way they acted.*

Irrational: *The world has to be a better place to live. There are too many bad things.*

Rational: *It is true that there are many bad things, but how many is too many? Too many means different things to different people. Don't forget that there are a lot of enjoyable things also.*

Some may argue about the effectiveness of clients arguing with themselves. Some find this technique peculiar because clients often do not agree with the rational belief. However, simply stating a belief has a persuasive influence on individuals *even if they disagree with the attitude.* Reciting the attitude out loud is even more influential.

Full Acceptance

To fully accept clients with all their difficulties and shortcomings has many advantages. Clients benefit from knowing that their therapist supports them fully in their attempts to change behavior patterns and thought processes.

Kids who originally were referred for an anger problem often develop additional neuroses related to their difficulties regarding the original problem. For example, students who are having a hard time overcoming an anger problem can become depressed over their lack of success. Some have referred to this phenomenon as *symptom stress,* when the anger at "C" becomes the "A" in depression.

A—Student is grounded for breaking curfew.
B—"My parents *shouldn't* be so strict. I *ought to* be able to stay out later like my friends."
C—Anger

The anger at point "C" now becomes a triggering event at point "A," which leads to self-denigration.

A—Student becomes angry over being grounded.
B—"There I go again making myself angry. *I can't do anything right! I am so worthless!* I'll never learn how to keep myself from getting angry."
C—Depression

When students are taught to accept themselves fully, along with their difficulties, they will be much less likely to spin into such a negative cycle.

Emotional Training

Ramsey (1974) described a technique he called *emotional training* that can be effective when a student is angry with another individual. Ask the student to recall pleasant experiences he/she has had with the individual with whom he/she is now angry. The student is to imagine all the pleasant exchanges he/she had with this individual until the warm, happy feelings overpower the angry, hostile feelings.

This intervention can be given as homework and may be effective at keeping a student from "stewing" and "ruminating" over negative feelings. In effect, this is reversing the process whereby intensely negative feelings are created. Rather than focusing on feelings of anger and hatred, the client is focusing on pleasant memories.

Rational Role Reversal (RRR)

Rational role reversal (RRR) helps deepen a client's conviction to rational thinking. In RRR, the client and therapist switch roles. The therapist explains why others have no right to talk behind his/her back, and the client tries to get the therapist to examine the rationality of his/her beliefs.

It is important to realize that clients can have an intellectual grasp of concepts but may not have an emotional understanding or commitment. They can recite the logic of the argument, but do not truly believe the disputation has merit. For lasting change to occur, clients need to adopt these new philosophies wholeheartedly. RRR can be of assistance in this regard.

Rational Story Telling Technique (RSTT)

The *rational story telling technique* (RSTT) is a simple and straightforward intervention that can be effective with younger children. Psychiatrist Richard Gardner uses the *mutual story telling technique,* but his approach is from a psychodynamic perspective. I developed the RSTT to incorporate the beneficial features of Gardner's work using REBT interventions.

As the name implies, RSTT involves having a child and therapist tell each other stories. The rules are that the child always goes first, and the story has to be made up and cannot come from a movie or television program.

The therapist listens to the story and looks for the irrational ideas contained within the tale. The therapist then tells his/her story, making it similar to the child's but replacing the irrational ideas with rational thoughts.

The following story was told to me by a client referred to me by his mother. She explained that Nick had numerous temper tantrums at home. He also occasionally experienced temper tantrums at school.

> **Nick:** *Once upon a time there was a big goat that lived in a forest. He liked to play with the other goats, but they didn't want to play with him. He got mad and butted the other goats with his horns, but they still wouldn't play with him. So he yelled and kicked and cried. The end.*

Obviously, the goat in the story was Nick. I told Nick the following story.

> **Therapist:** *My story is also about a big goat that lived in a forest. He also had problems making friends with other goats. Then one day he realized getting mad and butting the other goats wouldn't make the other goats like him. He also realized yelling and crying wouldn't make the other goats want to play with him.*
>
> *Instead he decided to ask the other goats nicely if he could join them in their game. If they said "no," he knew he didn't have to get mad. He could always play with other goats or by himself. It took a while, but the other goats found out that the big goat was fun to play with. They used to not like the way he butted them, but he didn't do that anymore. The goat was happy that he now had more friends to play with.*

Not all stories are lined up as perfectly with the presenting problem of anger. No matter what the child's story is about, the therapist always can incorporate a message that encourages the client to remain in control of his/her anger.

Chapter 9

TRANSCRIPTS FROM A CLIENT WITH ANGER PROBLEMS

This chapter contains transcriptions of three sessions with John, a 4th-grade male. He initially was referred to be in an upcoming anger control group, but due to the limited number of spaces available, John was not included in the group.

SESSION ONE

Therapist: *When we were walking down here, you said you got in trouble, and then I asked you a little bit about what happened there. So go ahead and start back with what you were saying.*

John: *OK. See I went to the bathroom, but they were being too loud, but Chris pushed me into the door, I mean into that thing that you. . . .*

T: *Paper towel?*

J: *Yeah, and I hit my head and I almost got in trouble for that but see, you're not allowed to go in the bathroom . . . or, if it's too loud you have to get out.*

Reprinted from *Anger Management in Schools: Alternatives to Student Violence*, Transcriptions, with permission from Technomic Publishing Company, Lancaster, PA.

T: *OK.*

J: *And see I went in it and I was trying to get out and Chris just goes, "Your mother is fat" and all that and Mrs. Townsend heard and. . . .*

T: *So you almost got in trouble for that.*

J: *And I go, I had to talk to Mrs. Swenson* (the principal), *and Mrs. Smith* (his teacher) *said, "Why don't you just let them go because I think they learned a lesson." That was me and Billy, Chris, and Tim and. . . .*

T: *So you didn't get in trouble, but you almost did. You were saying that, what teacher did you almost get in trouble with? Mr. Black?* (Author's Note: It became clear that this story was not leading anywhere, so I interrupted and tried to move the discussion to another topic. One of the advantages of REBT is that it is very problem focused and does not promote the notion that the therapist must listen to unproductive stories from the client. REBT practitioners are free to be very active with the client and direct the session where the therapist sees fit.)

J: *No, Smith.*

T: *Oh, but there was a different time. Not in the bathroom.*

J: *Uhm . . . what time was it?*

T: *That you might have to serve in detention.*

J: *That was Mrs. Swenson.*

T: *Mrs. Swenson . . . OK.*

J: *And she said to me and Tim because Chris had said, "Stay away from me," and he hit Billy with a baseball bat and Billy hit him back.*

T: *So you guys all got sent to the office.*

J: *Yeah, we all had to go talk to Mrs. Swenson. And she said me and Billy could go back to class because she thought we learned our lesson and we did.*

T: *Good.*

J: *Tim got an after school detention.* (Author's Note: I never did quite understand what went on with the baseball bat, paper towel holder, etc., but John was not bothered by what had transpired so I moved ahead once again.)

T: *What I wanted to talk to you a little bit about today is how some-times we get angry about stuff and that can lead to other kinds of problems. Now let me ask you, see if you can think back to a time when you got really angry about something. Something that happened in the last few days maybe or the last week or last month.*

J: *Last month when I got in trouble for my brother.*

T: *OK, tell me about that.*

J: *See, he was ripping up my baseball cards, and the cards were really good to me.* (Author's Note: I took that last comment to mean the cards were really important to John.) *And my mom said, "Stop him from doing that," and I got really angry and started calling him names.*

T: *Uh-huh, this is your little brother, right?*

J: *Yeah.*

T: *So you got really angry. Were you more angry at your mom or at your little brother?*

J: *I was more angry at my little brother.*

T: *Yeah, because he was ripping stuff up. Were you also angry be-cause you got in trouble and it wasn't really your fault?*

J: *Yeah.*

T: *Let me ask you about times here at school. Have you ever gotten into trouble here because you were really angry and you said some-thing or did something that you probably shouldn't have done?*

J: *People were playing soccer, you know, out by the tennis courts and they were using hands.*

T: *They were cheating?*

J: *And you're not supposed to use hands, and I said something in-appropriate like, "Knock it off, shut up" and all that and I got told on.* (Author's Note: I was very surprised to have a 4th-grader use the phrase "I said something inappropriate," but that was his choice of words.)

T: *So you didn't get in real trouble, but you were angry that they weren't playing the game the right way. That's not really fair that they were using their hands and stuff. What I want to try to help explain is that people think, I bet you think, that people using their hands and cheating at this game is what made you angry.* (Author's Note: At this point it is time to introduce the concept of the ABCs.)

J: *Yeah.*

T: *But you know what?*

J: *What?*

T: *Actually that's not quite right. It's something a little different. But that's what most people think, isn't it? Let me draw something here. We're going to say here at point "A" what happened was people were using their hands in soccer. How about we just put down people were cheating at soccer. Down here at point "C" you were really angry. OK? Now like I said, what most people think is that at point "A," people cheating at soccer, causes you to be angry at point "C." Actually there is a middle part, here at "B," that happens that actually makes you angry. But let me tell you a story to see if I can help explain this. Let's pretend you and I are going to go on a trip on a bus. Where are we going to go?*

J: *The Ozarks.*

T: *The Ozarks, all right, the Ozarks on a bus. So we're riding on a bus and you're sitting in the middle and I'm by the aisle, and there is somebody by the window. All of a sudden, for no reason, you get poked in the ribs. It's a real hard poke that really hurts.*

J: *Did he mean to poke me?*

T: *Let's not worry about that just now. How would you probably feel if you got poked in the ribs?*

J: *Mad.*

T: *OK. Good and mad and probably angry. So we put that down here at "C," and it's the same idea that we just talked about that people think getting poked in the ribs is what makes you angry. But now you're angry and your ribs hurt, and you turn over and you look and you see that it was a blind man and he was taking off his sweater because he was hot and he accidentally poked you right in the ribs because he couldn't see you. What do you think you'd feel at that point?*

J: *Sad.*

T: *Maybe sad. Why do you think you'd feel sad?*

J: *Because he's a blind person and he didn't mean to do it and probably felt bad for it.*

T: *Now you know what is really interesting is that getting poked in the ribs at point "A," that still happened, didn't it? But you feel two different ways at point "C," don't you? At first when you thought he did it on purpose, you were mad, weren't you? But then when you saw it was a blind man, you were sad because he didn't mean to and he's blind. Now you know what that shows us? There must be a middle part, "B," that changes to change how you feel? Do you understand me?*

J: *Yeah.*

T: *Explain it to me.* (Author's Note: As I've pointed out in the book, a client can say they understand but not be clear regarding a concept. It is always a good idea to check for understanding, especially when you are introducing important concepts.)

J: *There must be a middle part to make you feel two different things.*

T: *Right. Let's look at that a little closer. When you first got poked and were mad and angry, what could you have been thinking to yourself to make yourself angry about being poked in the ribs?*

J: *It was on purpose.*

T: *So it was on purpose.* (Author's Note: I write down the first part even though I know there's a second irrational belief that follows this initial statement. The belief "It was on purpose" is probably irrational as well because there is no proof that the poke was intentional.) *What are you saying to yourself about people poking people in the ribs on purpose? "He poked me in the ribs on purpose and. . . ."* (Author's Note: This is an example of the "complete the sentence" technique that can help clients find that second, irrational belief that can exist without the client's awareness.)

J: *I felt bad.*

T: *OK. Let me see if I can help. See if you can use this word to finish the sentence. Try to use the word "should" or "shouldn't" when you finish the sentence. He poked me in the ribs on purpose and. . . .*

J: *He shouldn't have done it.* (Author's Note: John was like a lot of clients. On their initial exposure to REBT, they need assistance finding the irrational belief. The goal is to help the client get to the point where he/she can do this easily without any outside assistance.)

T: *He shouldn't have done it. That's exactly right. Let me put that down. You know what? You know why I know that word "shouldn't" is real important? Because whenever we're getting really mad and angry do you know what is going on?*

J: *You shouldn't do it.*

T: (laughing) *What's really going on is that we're demanding that somebody act differently than they acted. Aren't we? When we say "He shouldn't have done it" aren't we kind of saying "I demand that he not do this?"*

J: *Yeah.*

T: *And you know the problem with that?*

J: *You're demanding something from other people and they might not agree with you.* (Author's Note: It is extremely rare for a 10-year-old to be able to spontaneously make a rational statement like John made

If clients don't catch on as quickly, therapists need not be alarmed. John was a good client to work with, and that's why I chose his sessions to use for the transcription portion of this chapter.)

T: *That's exactly right. Who controls how this guy on the bus acts? Do we?*

J: *No.*

T: *Who does?*

J: *Him.*

T: *He does, doesn't he? And whenever we demand that other people act a certain way, it's sort of like we're pretending to be god, isn't it? Sort of like we're going, "I am god, and I demand that you not do this." And like you said, we're not god and we don't control them. Now, here's the second part of this. You looked over and saw that he was a blind person, right? And you instantly thought something else. What did you probably think to make yourself feel sad or at least not be mad?*

J: *He was taking off his sweater, and he didn't mean to hit me.*

T: *Didn't mean to hit me.*

J: *It was an accident.*

T: *That's right. It was an accident. And you see how once you thought, "It was an accident," your anger went away right away, didn't it? Right away you said you felt sad instead of mad. Now let's take what we're talking about with the blind man and move it up here to people cheating at soccer. Remember, we're talking about people using their hands, which is against the rules and you got angry and mad. What do you think you were saying to yourself about people cheating that made you angry? See if you can use that word again.*

J: *That they shouldn't do it because that's cheating.*

T: *That's right. They shouldn't do it because that's cheating. That's really good. Now you know what? How could we change this demand, this shouldn't, to more of a wish or preference. Do you know what the* *word preference means? It's a big word and it sort of means if you had your choice between steak and pizza, which would you prefer?*

J: *Pizza.*

T: *OK, you'd choose pizza. So instead of saying "I demand steak or I demand pizza," you say "I would prefer to have pizza." How could we change that should or shouldn't into a preference; what kind of word could we use?*

J: *I'd prefer that they wouldn't use hands in soccer.*

T: (writing this down) *I'd prefer that they wouldn't use hands in soccer. Now can you see that the real difference between these two is that the shouldn't—"they shouldn't do it because that's cheating" —that's a commandment, isn't it? We talked about pretending we're god. But if you said, "I'd prefer that they wouldn't use hands in soccer," or do you know another word you could use? I wish they wouldn't.*

J: *That's what I was going to say.*

T: *You were going to say that? OK. I wish they wouldn't, but they can. Do you see how that would make you a lot less angry?*

J: *Yeah.*

T: *That's really good. You picked up on that really well. But I knew you would because you're a bright young man. Now which do you prefer, soccer or baseball?*

J: *I prefer both.*

T: *Good. You know what? Whenever you find yourself getting really angry about something, if you can stop and listen to what you are saying to yourself, I'll almost guarantee that there will be a "should" or a "must" or a "ought to" or a "have to" or any of those. If you can stop and listen to those, you know what? You won't be as angry. If you can change those "shouldn'ts" into words like "I wish" or "I prefer," or another phrase might be "It would be better if people didn't cheat in soccer, but people are going to do what they are going to do." It's sort of like it would have been better if Chris wouldn't have* *pushed you into the towel holder, but you or I or even Mrs. Swenson can't control what Chris does. Do you understand that?*

J: *Yep.*

T: *I think what we ought to do is get together next week and talk some more. Would you like that?*

J: *Yeah.*

T: *I want you to look for situations where you might make yourself angry, and try really hard to listen for those "shoulds" and "shouldn'ts" and see if you can't change them into "wishes." Can you try to do that?*

J: *Yes.*

Summary of Session One

John was a motivated client and picked up on the logic of REBT quickly. As I said, sessions don't always go this well, and this was especially enjoyable because it was the first time he had been introduced to these concepts. I recommend the following sequence of activities for the first session:

1. Ask the client for an anger problem or a situation where he/she is angered (i.e., identify and get the client to agree upon the "A").
2. Get the client to describe the emotion or "C."
3. Explain that "A" does not cause "C"; there is a middle part, "B."
4. Use "the blind man on the bus" story to illustrate that "B" causes "C."
5. Move the logic of "the blind man" to the problem the client presented.
6. Help the client identify the "B" that is causing anger.
7. Help the client change the IB into an RB.
8. Give the client a homework assignment to practice that helps him/her practice using his/her new RB.

SESSION TWO

T: *Do you remember what your homework assignment was for this week?*

J: *No.*

T: *It was to try to see, we were talking about anger. . . .*

J: *Oh, yeah, that's right.*

T: *Now do you remember?*

J: *Yeah.*

T: *See if you can tell me what your homework assignment was.*

J: *You told me to see if I could do what we talked about.*

T: *Right, I wanted you to try to think of a situation where you might normally have gotten angry and to keep yourself from getting angry.*

J: *Like I did on the soccer field.*

T: *Well let me hear about it. Tell me exactly what you did.*

J: *Well, I didn't say . . .*

T: *First tell me what happened, and then tell me what you did to keep from getting angry.*

J: *People were saying swear words when someone would score a goal or something and I said, "I wish you wouldn't say swears" and they just said, "OK." Then we played and I said, "I'll tell the teacher if you say swears," but I didn't get mad.*

T: *Right.*

J: *They just said things like, "Oh, shoot."*

T: *So not real swears?*

J: *Yeah.*

T: *But kind of like swears. So what did you do about that? What did you think?*

J: *I thought it was nice that they stopped it.*

T: *If they had continued to use swear words, what could you have thought to yourself to not make yourself angry?*

J: *I can always go tell the teacher.*

T: *OK, you could have told the teacher, but what could you have thought to yourself instead of thinking "they have to not swear" or "they shouldn't swear." What could you have thought to yourself?*

J: *They shouldn't swear.*

T: *OK, but if you use shouldn't, that's still a demand and you'd probably still get angry.*

J: *I wish.*

T: *I wish they wouldn't use swear words.*

J: *But it's their body and it's a free country.*

T: *That's right, and you know who controls their mouth and their voice? They do, don't they?*

J: *You can't go outside and talk it over and say "I'm going to quit this right now." See my dad smokes and he tried to quit and you know those pads that you put on your arm?*

T: *Yeah.*

J: *He went in the sun one day and it burned him. So he took it off. My mom and I wish he would quit it because it can lead to damage, but now when he smokes he goes outside.*

T: *So at least he doesn't smoke in the house.*

J: *Well, sometimes he does. But he goes in a different area.*

T: *You know what really impresses me? You realize that if your dad is going to smoke, he's going to smoke. You can either really, really upset yourself about that, which isn't going to change whether or not he smokes . . .*

J: *My mom used to smoke, but my brother coughed when she smoked. Then he would turn his nose up so my mom quit and I was really happy but that doesn't make my dad quit.*

T: *That's right. And like I was just saying, whether or not you upset yourself, is that going to make your dad quit?*

J: *No.*

T: *No, probably not.*

J: *My dad has tried to quit twice.*

T: *He's tried to, so maybe he will.*

J: *Have you ever seen an ashtray that can pull in the smoke?*

T: *Yes, I know what you mean.*

J: *We're trying to find one for him so he can smoke and be in the living room.*

T: *And it won't go all over the house. That's a good idea. I used to see those on television. Maybe you'll see a commercial with it on.*

J: *My mom is trying to find one.*

T: *It's really good that you're thinking clearly about this. If people want to swear on the soccer field, they're going to do that. You wish they wouldn't, but they have the right to. It's a free country like you said. And also what you're thinking about your dad smoking. "I wish he wouldn't. I hope he quits, but I'm not going to ruin my life worrying about this and demanding he quit." Who's the only person you can really demand anything from and expect to get something?*

J: *Me.*

T: *That's right.*

J: *I know I'm not going to smoke but I want to get an earring, though.*

T: *You want to get an earring. Do you think my earring looks good?*

J: *Yeah.*

T: *OK.*

J: *I really want to get an earring, but my dad won't let me.*

T: *Maybe when you're a little older.*

J: *He said if I get an earring I have to wear a dress to school.*

T: (laughing) *I was a lot older than you when I got an earring. I was in college.*

J: *My mom thinks I should be old enough to pay for my own earring. But I'm not using my college money.*

T: *That's probably not a good idea. My dad wasn't real happy when I got my earring either. But he got over it eventually.*

J: *I have enough money to go to college, and I don't want to spend it because I want to go to college so bad.*

T: *Well, if you really want to, then you probably will.*

J: *You know Larry Johnson? He could have played earlier but he stayed in college. I got the card of him when he was in college and I was really happy. I want to be like that.*

T: *You want to go to college.*

J: *Yeah, I want to be in the NBA just like Larry Johnson.*

T: *That sounds like a good goal to have. You know what is a good idea? To get a college degree just in case you don't make the pros. You can get a good job anyway.*

J: *Yeah, you can be a lawyer and get a Lamborghini. Did you know doctors can get any kind of car they want? The kind of car I want is a Lamborghini.*

T: *You have to make a lot of money to have one of those. You know what I'd like to know? How are you going to remember some of the* *lessons we learned? What are you going to do to think about those things over the summer?*

J: *I'll probably . . . I'm not sure.*

T: *Can you remind yourself when you get angry?*

J: *Yeah.*

T: *What will you think to yourself?*

J: *I'll think that every time they do something I don't like I'll try to think "I wish" instead of "he should."*

T: *Try to keep those "shoulds" from becoming too common, and keep them to wishes and preferences.*

J: *Yeah.*

T: *That will keep you a lot calmer. You won't have the same kind of problems with getting mad. That's a good goal to have. I'll probably see you one more time before the summer vacation, but if I don't, have a great summer. I'll see you for sure next fall because you'll be back and I'll be back. Let's get you back to class now because I don't want you to miss too much English.*

Summary of Session Two

John had an opportunity to practice his RB on the soccer field and seemed to do a pretty good job of remaining only irritated when the other players used swear words. He wanted to spend time talking about things such as his father's smoking and college plans, which are not related directly to the presenting problem. What I've found over the years is that students desire a few minutes of your time to talk about things other than the presenting problem. While REBT is very problem focused, that does not mean that a few minutes of a session can not be used to hear about the client's life in other areas that are unrelated to his/her difficulty. Remember, a majority of clients are not self-referred.

There are usually opportunities to reinforce REBT concepts even in an apparently unrelated story. Note that I tried to help John see that it wouldn't do any good to get angry about his father's smoking because his father was the person who was responsible for his smoking. His father either was going to stop smoking or he was not. John getting upset about his father's smoking would have very little impact on John's father's behavior.

SESSION THREE

T: *So what have you been up to since we talked last?*

J: *Not really nothing. I slept over at a friend's house Friday and Saturday.*

T: *Whose house?*

J: *Billy's.*

T: *Was that fun?*

J: *Yeah, he has a Nintendo.*

T: *I bet you played that all night.*

J: *Not really. We played basketball outside.*

T: *Now, do you play soccer in the summer?*

J: *Yes. Do you know if they are going to have the summer rec. program this summer?*

T: *I've heard that, but I'm not sure if that's true or not. I know there's going to be swimming. I know that for sure.*

J: *My mom said there was going to be basketball, baseball, and swimming. And maybe soccer and football.*

T: *Well, I hope they do offer all that.*

J: *But it's going to cost more money.*

T: *Yeah. That's what I've heard, too.*

J: *So my mom said I can only do three sports.*

T: *So you're only going to play your top three?*

J: *You know Arnold. He was the lifeguard at Booth Lake last summer, and he didn't think I could swim very good so he made me take a test. I passed it and now I can swim there whenever I want.*

T: *So now you can swim with everybody else?*

J: *Yeah, I can swim way out.*

T: *Good.*

J: *They thought I was too little.*

T: *Then you had to pass the test where you swim around the buoys for them?*

J: *Yeah.*

T: *Good.*

J: *Except I sort of cheated because the sand was so close to me when I was swimming that I kept on touching it so I kept on going.* (Author's Note: I tried to spend a short amount of time at the beginning of this session catching up on John's activities since our last visit.)

T: *You know what? What I wanted to talk about was what we talked about last time. About ways that we make ourselves angry. Can you tell me a little bit about what you remember that we talked about?*

J: *People cheating.*

T: *Right. People cheating at soccer and things like that. You were saying that when people use their hands and cheat and things like that, you'd get angry. What I'm wondering is, can you remember what you say to yourself to make yourself angry?*

J: *What was the question again?*

T: *Do you remember what you say to yourself to make yourself really angry? Do you remember that key word "should" or "shouldn't"?*

J: *They shouldn't do it because that's cheating.*

T: *Yeah. Remember how we talked about that's kind of a demand that people should do this or they shouldn't do that.*

J: *It's like pretending you're god and you're saying "The world has to be destroyed."*

T: *Right. Except instead of saying, "The world has to be destroyed," you're saying "People shouldn't cheat at soccer."*

J: *A lot of people do it though. It's kind of a free country, too.*

T: *What do you mean by that?* (Author's Note: I knew what John meant but it is helpful to get the client to verbalize his/her rational ideas.)

J: *People are free and they can do whatever they want.*

T: *It would be nice if people would do the right thing, wouldn't it?*

J: *A lot do the right thing.*

T: *That's right. But they don't have to, do they?*

J: *Because they're the best and they think they can do anything. Like Mike, he got adopted when he was five and now he has a mom and dad. Then he used his hands on the last goal and everybody was happy, but that was still cheating.*

T: *So they were happy even though he cheated to win. And you were kind of mad about that.*

J: *They say he can do anything.*

T: *Well, it is true that people can do what they want, pretty much. But it would be nice if people didn't cheat. Kind of like we said last time, "I wish they wouldn't use hands, but if they really want to they can anyway." Like you said, it's a free country and people can do* *what they want. Can you think of a time since the last time we talked where you've gotten angry about something other than soccer?*

J: *Like people swearing? People use the "S" word, the "F" word.*

T: *Right on the field, huh?*

J: *I know one kid who swears a lot.*

T: *So you end up feeling how about people swearing? Do you end up feeling angry?*

J: *Kind of.*

T: *Kind of angry.*

J: *I'm kind of used to it.*

T: *Let me ask you this. Listen real close because this is important. If you had to rate how angry you might feel if people swore, if you rated it between 0, which means not angry at all, and 100, how angry would you be?*

J: *About 50.*

T: *About 50. Let me ask you another question. How angry do you think it is OK to feel if people swear? What number would you give that? Do you understand what I mean?*

J: *Yeah. I'd rate it a little bit higher.*

T: *So you don't even get as angry as you think it's OK to get when people swear. Is that kind of what you are saying?*

J: *Yeah.*

T: *OK.* (Author's Note: The goal of this procedure is to determine if the client is angry or merely annoyed and irritated. I asked John first to rate how angry he was [50]. He then reported that he felt it would be appropriate to be even a little angrier than 50. Since his rating was below what he considered an appropriate level of anger, it is a pretty good indication that his response is appropriate for the situation. If clients reported that they would rate their anger at 85 and they felt an appropriate level would be 100 when people committed some misdeed, their thinking is still irrational. By stating that they consider 100 to be an appropriate response to some action, clients still are demanding that people not commit misdeeds. They still are demanding that people act the way the clients would like other people to act.)

J: *My mom would probably be at 100.*

T: *Your mom would be all the way to 100. She doesn't allow any swearing at all. That's probably a good idea. So what you're saying is that even though you get a little bit angry, it's a level of anger that you feel is about right for what happened. And it's OK to get a little bit angry. We call that irritated. Do you know what irritated means?*

J: *It means that you're sort of angry but not really angry.*

T: *Yeah. You're a little upset that people are acting in a way you don't like, but you're not really, really angry like you're ready to hit something.*

J: *It's like I'm bothered by it.*

T: *That's a good word. Bothered.*

J: *Because I don't like to hear other people talk that way, swearing and all that, like they think everybody talks like that.*

T: *You think they want you to swear.*

J: *They want everybody to act the same way as they act.*

T: *What would it mean if they decided that because you don't do what they want you to do, like you don't swear, do you think they would really stop liking you?*

J: *No.*

T: *Probably not. If they were really friends, they wouldn't stop liking you. Let me ask you this, now just pretend for a second, what if they stopped liking you? What would that prove about you?*

J: *I'd kind of be sad.*

T: *OK, you'd be sad because you might not have as many friends to play with. But let me ask you this. Would it mean that you're a rotten person?*

J: *No.*

T: *How come?*

J: *Because I don't want to say swears just because other kids do.*

T: *And that would just mean that you don't always go along with what everybody else does. That's OK.*

J: *My mom won't let me swear.*

T: *Sometimes other people just aren't going to like us. Wouldn't it be kind of boring if everybody liked us? Let me ask you this, can we do anything to make people like us?*

J: *Not really.*

T: *Probably not. And the really important part is that what other people think of us isn't as important as we sometimes make it out to be. Do you know what I mean? Can you explain what I mean by that?*

J: *Can you say that again?*

T: *Sure. What other people think of us isn't really as important as we make it out to be sometimes. Because we think, "If so and so doesn't like me, it means I'm a real nerd or a dork." And it really doesn't mean that, does it? See if you can explain that to me.*

J: *Just because somebody calls you a name you don't have to get mad about it.*

T: *You know what I say about that? If somebody called you a watermelon, it wouldn't make you a watermelon, would it? That's kind of silly, isn't it? If somebody calls you a dork, big deal.*

J: *It's a free country.*

T: *That's right. You don't have to get mad at all.*

Summary of Session Three

John appeared to be making good progress with his anger. The latter half of the session was spent assessing his self-acceptance. Many students feel that if others don't accept them, they can't accept themselves. John did not appear to suffer from this need for approval, which was a positive indicator for his overall emotional development.

PART D
ANXIETY

Chapter 10

ANXIETY

Children and adolescents with anxiety disorders will be increasingly prevalent as we approach the twenty-first century. This generation has grown up in an environment filled with dangers that earlier generations did not have to consider. Here are but a few examples of the stressors that surround kids and contribute to anxiety disorders:

- Approximately 2,000 adolescents are arrested annually for murder.
- Approximately 34,000 adolescents are arrested annually for aggravated assault.
- The murder rate per 100,000 for white males was 3.8 in 1950. By 1988 it had risen to 7.9. For black males, the murder rate for the same period rose from 58.9 to 101.8.
- One in five students carries a weapon to school at least once a month.
- For every gun in school, there are seven (7) knives brought to school.
- The current divorce rate is between 40% and 50%.
- There are 2.5 million more children below the poverty level today than in 1980.
- The average work week went from under 41 hours in 1973 to nearly 47 hours in 1989.

To put this in REBT terms, children and adolescents have a lot of "A's" (events, situations) that can and do lead to anxiety and fear. It is important to point out that anxiety and fear are different emotions and will not be used interchangeably.

Fear is an emotional response to the threat of harm, injury, or loss. *Anxiety*, on the other hand, can be defined as an emotional response to *perceived* dangers that seem real but which are mainly imaginary because so little probability of occurrence exists.

If the chances of a feared event occurring are minimal, the emotion probably is referred to appropriately as anxiety. For example, a child who is too concerned to drink a glass of milk because there might be germs in the milk is suffering from anxiety. While it is theoretically possible for harmful germs to be in the milk, the probability is quite remote.

Anxiety, like depression and anger, is not caused by events but by the view children have of events. That is not to say that children would not be appropriately *concerned* about the separation of their parents or the rise of violence in their schools. Being concerned about an unpleasant situation will increase children's ability to act in a manner to ensure their health and happiness. When that concern turns into extreme anxiety, children can become obsessed with the situation or paralyzed into inactivity. In such cases, they are less happy, less healthy, and less able to reach their goals.

If anxiety were caused by events, then everyone would be anxious about the same events. For example, everyone would be anxious about speaking in public. As we know, not every student is anxious about public speaking and some even enjoy it.

The core irrational belief associated with anxiety usually is made up of both a rational and an irrational belief. For example, students who are anxious to speak in front of the class probably are thinking something such as, "I might make a mistake," which is entirely rational. It is possible for students to make any number of mistakes such as forgetting what they were going to say or making an embarrassing error. The second part of their self-talk probably will contain a belief such as, "I might make a mistake *and that would be horrible, awful, and terrible. I couldn't stand it if that happened.*" This second portion is irrational and causes the anxiety. The second portion is an exaggeration of the repercussions of making a mistake. As Ellis often stated, it's taking a *hassle*, and turning it into a *horror.*

To make a mistake is not horrible, awful, and terrible; it's merely unfortunate. Words like horrible, awful, and terrible exaggerate an event's "badness" and turn an inconvenience into a catastrophe. Life has many inconveniences but very few catastrophes.

REBT practitioners have pointed out that by believing an event is horrible, awful, and terrible, the client is perceiving the event to be "worse than 100% bad." This is what Ellis has called *magical thinking* and is clearly beyond reality. Things can be bad, and maybe even very bad, but they are never more than 100% bad which is the implication of evaluations such as horrible, awful and terrible.

Anxiety also is created by the irrational belief that if a feared event were to occur, it would be so bad that the client would be unable to "stand it." The thought "I couldn't stand it" is irrational because it is not verifiable and simply untrue. If the student giving the speech were to make a mistake, the student *would* stand it because he/she would have no choice but to stand it! To say "I couldn't stand it" literally means, "If the feared event were to occur, I would die." No one ever died from making a mistake while speaking in public. Many have been embarrassed, but public humiliation never has been terminal. If it were, we all surely would have perished long ago.

Strict behavioral psychologists such as Skinner have proposed that anxiety is the result of a learned association between an event (or in their terms, a stimulus) and the emotional reaction (response) to that event. If a child became frightened on an elevator, he/she learned to associate the feeling of fear with elevators. A behavioral explanation would state that the frightening experience on an elevator is responsible for the anxiety. Thus, the association between the stimulus and response is causing the anxiety. While this appears to be an adequate explanation, it is not explain adequately what is transpiring in the situation.

The anxiety actually is caused by something happening *between* the stimulus and response. In that split second between the stimulus and response, clients think about and evaluate the stimulus. Strict behaviorists want to ignore the fact that something happens *in the person* between the stimulus and the response. In REBT terms, behaviorists want to leave out the "B" (the belief) and go from "A" (the activating event) directly to "C" (the consequence or emotion).

Many children have frightening experiences on roller coasters but do not avoid roller coasters and even stand in line for hours to ride them. The difference between their reactions to roller coasters and elevators has to do with their beliefs. After riding both, children may have the rational belief "That was scary." The child who is *anxious* over riding the roller coaster believes "That was scary and *I can't stand it,*" whereas the roller coaster enthusiast enjoyed the experience because he/she believes "That was scary—let's do it again!"

Another reason the strict behavioral view does not do an adequate job of explaining anxiety (and conditioning in general) has to do with so-called *one exposure* or *single case associations*. Some events are so powerful that after a single exposure a person is said to be conditioned. (In most situations, it takes numerous associations between a stimulus and response to produce an association.) A child can be so frightened of elevators after only one ride that he/she will do anything to avoid elevators in the future. Has conditioning occurred after only one exposure, or is something else responsible for the anxiety? Once again, the answer is found at point "B."

It is not that the association has been learned after one exposure to the elevator. In the passing days and years there will be hundreds, if not thousands, of associations between the feeling of anxiety and the elevator. The important distinction is that *these associations occur in the child's mind*. Over the years, the anxiety over the elevator is maintained by reliving and rethinking the event. Each time the thought occurs there is a reindoctrination of the belief, "That was scary and I can't stand it." The child is conditioned, but not by the strength of the one exposure to the elevator. He/she is conditioned by reliving the event in his/her mind. The ABC analysis would look like this:

A—Riding on an elevator.
B—"That was scary and I can't stand it."
C—Anxiety.

By continually believing that he/she could not stand the elevator, the child maintains and even strengthens the phobia. If the child were to challenge and dispute the irrational belief (IB), he/she would have the opportunity to face the fear.

A—Riding on an elevator.
B—"That was scary and I can't stand it."
C—Anxiety.
D—"Where is the proof that I can't stand riding an elevator? Just because I feel nervous does not mean I can't stand it. I'm not going to die from riding an elevator. The fact is, I can stand it."
E—Concern, slightly nervous.

As has been discussed, it is important to try to decide with the client if a fear is appropriate or exaggerated. The following technique can be beneficial in that regard:

Therapist: *On a scale from 1 to 100, with 1 being not anxious at all and 100 being the most anxious, what would you say would be an appropriate level of anxiety for a ride on an elevator?*

Ed: *For just a normal elevator and not one of those glass elevators?*

T: *Right, just a normal elevator.*

E: *Probably about 10 to 15.*

T: *OK, 10 to 15. And what would you rate your level of anxiety about riding an elevator?*

E: *Probably about 40 or 50.*

T: *So you agree that your level is too high.*

E: *Yes, I'm way more nervous about it than most people. I'll walk up 10 flights of stairs to avoid riding one of those things.*

In the Chapter 11, interventions and disputations for use with clients who are suffering from anxiety will be presented. The very best way to overcome anxiety is to *do the thing that you fear*. The interventions in Chapter 11 have more emphasis on behavioral techniques than do the disputations suggested for use for anger (Chapter 8) and depression (Chapter 14).

DISPUTATIONS AND INTERVENTIONS WITH ANXIOUS CLIENTS

REBT uses cognitive, behavioral, and emotive techniques to help clients examine their thoughts and find the errors in their thinking. Following are samples of interventions that can be applied to clients who suffer from anxiety problems.

COGNITIVE TECHNIQUES

As was stated earlier, the goal of most cognitive techniques is to encourage clients to question the logic of their beliefs (Walen et al., 1980). It is hoped that clients will learn to always "have their meter running" and be more aware of their thinking.

Human beings are continually thinking, even if they are unaware of their thoughts. Clients can learn to be careful monitors of their thoughts, which has many advantages in the course of therapy. It is difficult for clients to apply the skills they learn in therapy outside of counseling if they are unable to access their private talk.

Use of Exaggeration

Anxiety is produced by exaggerations of an event's "badness." The intentional use of exaggerations is one of the most effective means of helping clients understand how their exaggerations cause anxiety.

99

Therapist: *So you are worried that you may not get an A on the project, which will drop your grade a half letter grade?*

Brehan: *Yes, and if I don't get an A, I'd drop out of the top 10% of the class.*

T: *Wow, that is gruesome. Do you think your parents would still let you live with them?*

B: *Well, sure. It's not that big a deal.*

T: *Isn't it? You're making it sound like a catastrophe. If you were to drop out of the top 10%, do you think you could still manage to find just a little bit of happiness?*

B: *Yes, I guess I am making kind of a big deal out of this.*

Assume the Worst

Another effective technique involves asking clients a very simple question: *"What's the worst that could happen?"* Once clients have thought through the situation logically, they will see their feelings of panic are usually unnecessary because rarely are there "life and death" struggles being waged. However, it is possible for clients to *feel* as though a situation is "life and death" because of their exaggerated thinking.

Therapist: *It sounds like you are really terrified of going to the dentist for that examination?*

Drew: *I am terrified because they are going to clean my teeth and I hate that. It hurts and my gums bleed. They might find a cavity.*

T: *That's true, they could find a cavity. But really, what's the worst thing that could happen?*

D: *I'd have to get a filling.*

T: *Have you ever had a filling?*

D: *Yes. I've got four of them.*

T: *So you sort of remember what it was like, and I know it's not a heck of a lot of fun. But what's the worst thing that could happen?*

D: *I'd have to get a filling and it might hurt.*

T: *That's right, you'd be uncomfortable, maybe even in pain, for a little while; then it would be over. You've been uncomfortable hundreds of times before, and you've never died from it. You're taking this from being a pain in the behind, make that a pain in the tooth, and turning it into a gigantic problem. Do you see how you're making it worse than it really is?*

In almost every instance, the imagination of an event is worse than the reality. The fear of the event is more uncomfortable than the actual event.

Cognitive Distraction

A distraction technique that can be used anywhere involves having the client think of either the funniest or happiest memory he/she has. The memory is best if it can bring an instantaneous smile or laugh to a client.

Instruct the client that when he/she is starting to feel himself/herself becoming anxious, he/she is to immediately picture the preselected scene. There are certain clients who are quite successful with this technique.

BEHAVIORAL TECHNIQUES

Reinforcement

The use of reinforcement is encouraged with many problems previously discussed in this book and also can be used with anxious clients. In fact, using rewards to encourage clients to do the very things they fear is often quite helpful.

A 7-year-old was experiencing anxiety over attending a new school and would complain of bellyaches each morning before she came to school. One morning the parents allowed her to stay home because they believed she might really be sick. It is impossible to say for certain whether her stomach hurt, but according to her parents, she did not have a fever.

The next morning she was hysterical and did not want to get on the school bus. The mother called, and I convinced her to do whatever was needed to get the child to school. The longer she stayed out of school, the harder it would be to get her back.

The parents agreed on a plan to allow the child to earn points each day she attended school without complaining, begging, and crying. Once she had 10 points, she could pick out a toy she had been wanting. The chart was kept on the refrigerator, and the parents gave her a lot of praise and encouragement when she did well in addition to the points. As is the case with most school phobia, once a few school days are completed successfully, the child was fitting in well at her new school.

Systematic Desensitization

Behavioral psychologist Joseph Wolpe pioneered this technique to overcome anxiety. Clients are to make a list of situations or events in which they experience anxiety. The list is made in a hierarchy from "mild" to "severe." Clients then are taught to imagine the least threatening situation. When they begin to feel anxious, they are to interrupt their anxiety by switching to a preselected relaxing image. Their anxiety will dissipate because the states of anxiety and relaxation cannot exist simultaneously.

Once clients are able to think of the least threatening situation without becoming anxious, they are to move to the next event on the hierarchy while performing the series of imagination/relaxation techniques. The process is repeated with each anxiety provoking situation.

Once clients have worked through the entire hierarchy and have succeeded in remaining calm rather than becoming anxious, they will have been desensitized to the anxiety provoking situation. Clients seem to have gathered "evidence" that they can experience a feared event, albeit only mentally, and a catastrophe does not follow.

In Vivo Desensitization

For some clients, mentally desensitizing themselves to a feared event will be insufficient to overcome their anxiety. They will need to face the anxiety *in vivo* (through life). *In vivo desensitization* involves actually facing the feared situation rather than merely imagining the event.

The quickest way to get over an anxiety is to actually do the thing that one fears. Once a child faces the feared situation, he/she learns that nothing horrible is going to happen and he/she becomes desensitized.

Sounds easy, right? It is not . . . because the anxious person will go to nearly any lengths to avoid the event or situation he/she fears. There are stories of agoraphobics (those fearful of open spaces) staying inside their homes for years at a time by getting others to do their shopping and take care of their responsibilities.

Therapists can accompany clients as they encounter the situation to be supportive during the in vivo desensitization. Counselors can remind clients to use their rational coping statement during the experience and generally provide reassurance during this difficult time.

Also an advisable procedure is to set up rewards that clients can earn if they face their anxiety. Once again, anxiety disorders only can be considered mastered when clients can face the situations in life. Any incentives counselors can provide to bring about this end are recommended.

EMOTIVE TECHNIQUES

Rational Emotive Imagery (REI)

REI has been discussed previously as a means of helping clients produce their own rational belief (RB) rather than relying on a therapist-produced RB. REI is particularly well-suited to be used with anxious clients.

REI allows clients to mentally experience the event in the safety of their home or the therapist's office. If the images become too much for them, clients are always aware that they are in complete control and can mentally leave the scene in their mind.

Time Projection

An effective technique from Lazarus (1978) that can be beneficial in disputing irrational beliefs is *time projection*. When a client is anxious about an upcoming event, he/she often does not consider the fact that life will continue *after* the event. The purpose of time projection is to get the client to imagine the world after the "dreaded event" has occurred.

If an adolescent is extremely anxious about a test that is approaching, encourage the student to imagine a month, two months, or a year in the future.

How much of an impact will this test have on life in the future? Chances are the student will not even remember the test and, therefore, it is not worth losing sleep over. By realizing that this test is a time limited inconvenience, the client might be able to keep the test's importance in perspective.

Forceful Dialogue

With this disputation, clients are encouraged to argue forcefully with themselves regarding their irrational beliefs.

> **Irrational:** *I can't ask out Jessica because she might turn me down and that would prove what a loser I am.*
>
> **Rational:** *Just because she might turn me down doesn't mean I would be a total loser. It would just mean she doesn't want to go out on a date with me.*
>
> **Irrational:** *But I'd feel humiliated and I couldn't stand that.*
>
> **Rational:** *Of course I could stand it. I've felt humiliated before and haven't died. Besides, I'd only feel humiliated if I thought I were somehow less than adequate.*
>
> **Irrational:** *But then I wouldn't have a date for the party and that would be the worst thing ever.*
>
> **Rational:** *It would be unfortunate if I didn't have a date, but the earth wouldn't stop rotating. I probably could still have a good time at the party without a date.*

This technique can be practiced with the client during therapy sessions. Counselor and client take turns being the rational and irrational voice—this is similar to another emotive technique called *rational role reversal.*

Rational Role Reversal (RRR)

RRR has been discussed previously and is valuable because it helps deepen a client's conviction to rational thinking. RRR involves having the client and therapist switch roles. The therapist tells the client what the client became anxious about, and the client's job is to dispute the irrational ideas put forth by the therapist. Refer to the chapter on interventions with depressed clients (Chapter 14) if more detailed information is required.

Assertiveness Training

Helping students learn to stand up for themselves is included as an anxiety intervention because many times shyness is the result of anxiety. Clients are afraid that if they assert themselves others may not like their behavior and reject them.

As with many situations, this first portion of a client's belief ("They may not like it if I tell them what I think") is rational. The belief that the client "couldn't stand" being rejected is anxiety producing. This irrational belief then can be disputed and, hopefully, the student will come to realize that if others did not like him/her, it would not be a catastrophe. Almost no one enjoys being rejected, but many can learn to accept it as a part of life and not make themselves miserable.

Rational Story Telling Technique (RSTT)

The following story was told to me by a 7-year-old who was anxious whenever she was out of contact with her mother. The child had lost several significant others in her life, and her mother was about the only person left.

> **Sara:** *Once upon a time there was a princess who was nervous about her queen. She was afraid that the queen was going to die and leave her all alone and she wouldn't know what to do. If the queen died, the princess would have to go to a foster home. She was afraid of going to a foster home.*

The child obviously was projecting her fears into her story. Her mother reported that the child would knock on the door when the mother was in the bathroom just to make certain she was all right. I told Sara this story.

> **Therapist:** *Once upon a time there was a prince who loved his father, the king, very much. The prince was afraid something would happen to the king, so the prince worried all the time. He worried so much it made his stomach hurt.*
>
> *Then one day he thought about it and decided he was going to stop worrying because it didn't do any good. He knew the king was prob-*

ably not going to die for a long, long time. Even if the king did die, the prince would be able to have someone to take care of him. There would still be some people who would love him and take care of him. So he decided to have fun instead of worry. The end.

Shame Attacking Exercises

This intervention encourages clients to behave deliberately in a somewhat unusual manner in hopes of helping them lose their self-consciousness. Clients must realize that it is not a horror if others think clients are acting foolishly. As REBT therapists point out to their clients, no one *is* a fool for *acting* foolishly! People even can learn to have some fun with this.

I was at a conference with Dr. Ellis a few years ago, and he challenged all attendees to commit some act that they normally might feel ashamed of doing. The key was to try not to feel anxious and ashamed of their "shameful" behavior. One man ran through the lobby of the hotel screaming, "I'm rich, I'm rich, I'm fabulously wealthy!" Someone else broke into song on an elevator full of strangers.

These types of activities are an excellent means of proving to clients that they will not die from embarrassment. They will be open to engage in new experiences instead of being limited due to self-imposed concerns over others' opinions of them.

Chapter 12

TRANSCRIPTS FROM AN ANXIOUS CLIENT'S SESSIONS

The following transcription is of two sessions I had with a 17-year-old junior girl who shall be called Monica. We had worked together in a group for students who were having family difficulties so we knew each other very well. I also had worked two or three sessions with her a few months before these sessions took place.

SESSION ONE

Therapist: *Monica, good to see you. How have you been since group ended?*

Monica: *Pretty good. I've been busy applying to colleges and getting financial aide stuff sent out.*

T: *Are you applying for any scholarships?*

M: *Yes. I'm not sure how many. A couple of them are those big ones like the Elks. You know that one.*

T: *No.*

M: *It's got an essay and you have to get letters of recommendation from a minister and a lot of stuff.*

T: *Lots of work.*

M: *Yeah, but it pays a lot. I can't remember but it's something like five scholarships total and each are worth $5,000.*

T: *Have you decided on a school for sure yet?*

M: *Not really, but I think it's either going to be Madison or Concordia.*

T: *Sort of big school vs. small school.*

M: *Yeah. I think I'd like to go to Concordia but the cost is a lot more than Madison. Plus my brother went to Madison.*

T: *How about a major? I know you've been thinking about biology, or pre-med I should say, or psychology.*

M: *That's kind of why I wanted to talk to you. Can you tell me how long it would take me to be a psychologist?*

T: *That sort of depends on what kind of a psychologist you want to be. If you want to be a school psychologist like me, the minimum amount of school is about six years, and lots of school psychologists have more. If you want to be a clinical psychologist, that's probably about eight years and maybe nine.*

M: *Nine years!*

T: *Part of that you'd be out working "in the field," as they call it, and you might be making a little bit of money. I'm really not that certain, but I have some friends who got to do paid internships. It wasn't like they made a lot of money, but they did have some money to live on while they were in school.*

M: *That's what scares me.*

T: *Not having any money.*

M: *No. The amount of time. That's like half as long as I've been alive. The worst part is, what if I don't like it.*

T: *I used to feel kind of like that. Because you're right, there are no guarantees that you'll like the job after you're out. Is that something you're really worried about?*

M: *Yes. I've been stuck trying to pick a major and I can't make up my mind because I'm afraid I'll make the wrong choice.*

T: *You know you don't have to pick a major for a while. I actually didn't declare a major until my second year in college, and then when I was a junior, I declared a second major.*

M: *But what if I never can make my mind up?*

T: *Let me ask you this. Let's get right to the root of your fears. What if you picked a major and you found out that you didn't like it. Or even worse, you went all the way through school and found out that you hated your job.*

M: *That's more of what I'm afraid of than anything. That I'd find out too late.*

T: *What would be the worst thing that would happen?* (Author's Note: This is what Ellis has referred to as "the elegant solution." The attempt is to assume the worst and go after the irrational beliefs associated with such situations.)

M: *Then I'd have wasted all that time and money.*

T: *Would it really be a waste? Wouldn't you still have something to show for it?*

M: *Well I'd have something, but it wouldn't be a lot to show for nine years of work.*

T: *So again, what would be the worst thing that would happen?*

M: *I guess I'd have to change careers or go back to school or something.*

T: *That's pretty accurate, I would guess. Now let me ask you this. Would that be a tragedy?*

M: *Not really a tragedy.*

T: *Of course not. Why not?*

M: *Because I would have learned a lot, hopefully. By then and I'd have probably other opportunities by then.*

T: *Right. Do you see how thinking about it like that makes you feel a little more calm? I guess I should ask you, does it make you feel better thinking about it that way?*

M: *Yes. I don't feel so . . . what's the word . . . frantic.*

T: *Good, because number 1, I don't think that's going to happen to you—that you'd get through and find that you hate it—and number 2, it really wouldn't be a waste.*

M: *What do you mean? If I went to school and majored in something that I found out I didn't like, it wouldn't be a waste?*

T: *Well, it would depend on how you define waste. I define waste, I guess, as using something and not getting any use from it or any value from it.*

M: *Yeah, that's what I mean too because it wouldn't be getting any value from a major if I decided I wanted to do something else.*

T: *But that's where I think we disagree. Wouldn't you still be getting some value out of the knowledge you would have from the classes and stuff?*

M: *Oh . . . I was thinking of the money from the job I would get afterwards.*

T: *I know, but there are things you get out of school other than a chance to get a job after you get out. In fact, I think the most important things you get have nothing to do with your job.*

M: *I was thinking only of career stuff.*

T: *If you changed your ideas about the value of a major pertaining to more than just career stuff, you might not be so uptight about it.*

M: *I just was thinking it would be a complete waste of time to go to school for nine years and then decide you don't want to do that.*

T: *First off, don't make this worse than it already is. You're assuming that those nine years will be nothing but hard work. They'll probably be the best time of your life. In fact, I'd be willing to bet you that you'll have more fun in college than when you get out and become "terminally important."*

M: *"Terminally important?" Where'd you get that?*

T: *That's something my friend Danae said to me a long time ago, and I've always remembered it. She said, "Have some fun before you become terminally important like the rest of the world." Let me tell you something Monica, this grown-up stuff isn't all that great. Taxes, jobs—don't worry, they will be here waiting for you when you're ready.*

M: *So you had a lot of fun in college?*

T: *Oh yeah. And you will too. I see lots of people today who will do almost anything to stay in college because it is a lot of fun. Let's get back to the idea that if you decide to change your major or if you don't like your job it would be a complete waste of time. Again, would it really be a complete waste of time?*

M: *No, I guess you're right.*

T: *Do you see how you're making it seem that way by thinking about it as a tragedy?*

M: *I'm making too much out of it. Is that what you're saying?*

T: *That's exactly what I'm saying. It probably won't happen, and if it did, you'd still have many, many benefits from the degree that will benefit you in what you decide to do next.*

M: *In psychology you mean?*

T: *Or biology or whatever. You're going to learn how to be a better thinker and better writer and a wiser person. How can that be a waste of time?*

M: *I guess you're right. My mom says I'm too focused on the future and my career and things like that.*

T: *Like I told you, those things will be there waiting for you.*

M: *Thanks for your advice. I'm going to try to remember what you said and not worry about it so much.*

T: *You know one last thing to think about. I don't see how you can make a bad choice. Concordia or Madison . . . both are good schools and have a lot to offer. Psych or biology . . . there is lots of good stuff to learn in either of those. You might even think about majoring in one and minoring in the other.*

SESSION TWO

The next session took place three weeks after the first session. Monica stopped me in the hall and said she wanted to talk for a few minutes because she had reached some decisions.

M: *Got your recorder going?*

T: *Yes. So what's it going to be?*

M: *I'm pretty sure I'm going to go to Madison, but I found out last week that I've been accepted at both.*

T: *You didn't think you wouldn't get in, did you, with your GPA?*

M: *I thought I'd get in, but you never know for sure until it's official.*

T: *So it's going to be Madison, but you've got Concordia as a backup just in case something doesn't go quite right with Madison.*

M: *Right, and I think I'm going to declare a psych major but take a biology course or two to see if I like it.*

T: *That's not a bad idea because most schools have a science requirement and you can use your bio class to fill that requirement.*

M: *Plus, I think you're right that I can't really make a bad decision because whichever way I go I'll have opportunities.*

T: *The other thing is that most people change there major something like 2.3 times in college.*

M: *2.3? What do you mean?*

T: *That's just the average—between two and three times.*

M: *Oh, I see what you mean now. I didn't understand at first.*

T: *So you're feeling OK about things for now?*

M: *Yeah, because I'm not going to go crazy about it, at least for now. It's like you used to say in group—don't sweat the small stuff and it's all small stuff.*

T: *You know that's not totally true. Some things aren't small stuff, but most things people feel all worried about are small stuff.*

M: *I have to get to lunch or I won't be able to get to class on time. Thanks again.*

T: *Sure. See you later.*

PART E
DEPRESSION

Chapter **13**

DEPRESSION
AND LOW SELF-ESTEEM

An article appearing in *USA Today* (1992, December 2, p. 1) reported that depression is continuing to rise in America. The article also stated that the rate of depression has increased with each passing generation since records started being kept around the turn of the century. Mental health experts cited in the article stated that the depression problem was "nearing epidemic proportions." Estimates regarding the hundreds of millions of dollars lost annually due to depression-related work absences and lowered productivity also were reported.

The epidemic may be even greater among our nation's youth. As part of my dissertation (Wilde, 1993b), 80 high school students were given the *Beck Depression Inventory* (BDI). Of these 80 randomly selected high school students, 25% were found to be at least mildly depressed. Several scored in the moderate and severe range of depression according to the BDI.

Suffering from childhood depression increases the likelihood of depression in adulthood. Depression not only affects an individual's mood and life satisfaction but has other long-term social consequences as well.

McGuire (1990) studied 46 dysthymic (mildly depressed) women who were matched with control subjects who had no psychiatric diagnoses. The mildly depressed group had significantly fewer friends and social contacts. The dysthymic patients also had significantly lower incomes and significantly less living space per household. It appears from the research that not only do depressed clients

117

suffer emotionally, but they also suffer socially, economically and with regards to household comfort.

Another topic related to depression and applicable and relevant for all students is self-esteem. There are thousands of books designed to raise a child's self-esteem and hundreds of packaged programs attempting to do the same. Educators, parents, and the general public all appear to have a sincere interest in this issue. To recognize that the problem of low self-esteem has received so much attention is not surprising. Many of the social ills that plague our country have been blamed on poor self-esteem. Drug use/abuse, teenage pregnancy, and juvenile crime all are reported to be related to self-esteem or the lack there of.

While some reports in the late 1980s found adolescent drug use to be on the decline, the most recent reports in the spring of 1994 indicated that drug use is again on the rise. There are still millions of children and adolescents using illegal drugs. No matter how you paint it, drug use is still a major concern.

Use of certain drugs (cocaine) does appear to have had moderate decline, but other drugs (LSD and heroin) are regaining popularity. Use of the drug that leads to other drug use (often called a "gateway" drug) also is increasing. Any guesses which drug I am referring to? The number one gateway drug is nicotine.

Feelings of low self-worth are related to the decision to experiment with drugs. It is hard to believe that teenagers who are comfortable with themselves would be pressured into smoking crack, dropping LSD, and sticking needles into their arms. Many adolescents who abused substances have told me that it is not the physical effects of the drugs they enjoyed as much as the danger and excitement of doing something they knew was "wrong" and against the law. Many felt like they would be accepted if they dabbled in drugs. This is where the issue of self-esteem comes into play.

Kids who can accept themselves readily do not have to resort to dangerous (not to mention illegal) activities to fit into a peer group. As Dr. Ellis has stated, *"High self-esteem is just a fancy way of saying you're not overly concerned with what others think of you."* People who use drugs just because they want to fit in obviously care too much what others think.

Teenage sexual activity and the resulting pregnancies also are related to feelings of low self-worth. Human beings are gregarious by nature, but never is this more apparent than in adolescence when the desire to belong to a group becomes intensified. Kids will do nearly anything to fit in, even if that means surrendering their bodies. Those who feel unconnected and unloved will search for and eventually find that sense of belonging somehow.

It has been said that girls use sex to get love and boys use love to get sex. The adolescent female gives into the pressure to have sex oftentimes because she is afraid she will lose her boyfriend. The adolescent male will tell his girl-friend he loves her to convince her to have sex.

Juvenile crime may seem to be unrelated to self-image, but a very strong connection exists between the two. In fact, the staggering increase in violent crime is partially the result of the loss of respect for human life. This loss of respect is not only in regards to the victim but also pertains to the perpetrator. How could juvenile criminals murder a person if they had the least amount of respect for the basic rights of the victim? How powerless and ineffective must someone feel that he/she would resort to killing another human being in order to gain a sense of mastery over the world? *If adolescents do not value their own lives, they cannot value others'.*

Adolescents who have low self-esteem or suffer from depression tend to define themselves as "rotten," "worthless," and "no damn good." All people have a basic predisposition to behave in a manner that is consistent with their beliefs about themselves. This holds true whether the self-thoughts are positive or negative. If kids believe they are "bad," they will act in a manner to confirm this belief. The manifestation of this belief can be demonstrated easily through crime.

The term *cognitive dissonance* has been used to describe this phenomenon. Cognitive dissonance refers to the mild feelings of anxiety that arise when a person's beliefs about self and his/her behaviors are incongruent. When children define themselves as "good" and act otherwise, they will feel a mild sense of anxiety. They then will try to eliminate these feelings of anxiety by either (1) changing their beliefs about themselves or (2) changing their behavior. Since it is much easier for kids to change their actions than their self-images, it is usually the behavior that changes.

As was stated above, an individual with negative self-image will act in a manner consistent with that belief. Quite simply, kids who think of themselves as "bad" will commit crimes or other "bad" behavior to reaffirm their beliefs.

SELF-ACCEPTANCE

REBT prefers to use the term *self-acceptance* rather than self-esteem. This may seem like mere semantics, but an important distinction can be drawn between the two terms.

Self-acceptance refers to the act of accepting oneself regardless of significant accomplishments and/or serious mistakes. The concept of self-acceptance implies that there is an understanding that a difference exists between *who you are* and *what you do*. For example, individuals can have deficits or weaknesses but still value and accept themselves as fallible human beings. People are much too complicated to be given a total rating based on one or a few attributes. Helping kids learn to accept themselves as they are, with all their positive *and* negative traits, is an important and requisite step in kids thinking and behaving rationally.

Self-esteem, as it is commonly thought of today, refers to valuing, esteeming, or thinking highly of oneself. Implied in this concept is the belief that people deserve to feel good about themselves *only* when they have done something worthwhile. In effect, people are required to earn their esteem. Under the current definition of self-esteem, children are not supposed to feel good about themselves just because they are alive. Some would even find that feeling downright conceited.

A tremendous amount of emotional suffering has been caused by the idea that individuals can accept themselves only when they have achieved something worthwhile. These are strong words, but let me explain how the current conceptualization of self-esteem has caused millions of kids to feel they are less than they *should* be. A simple, yet accurate definition of low self-esteem is the feeling experienced when people believe they are less than they should be.

When children and adolescents are succeeding and feeling positively about themselves, the above mentioned misconceptions about self-esteem cause only minor problems. If children believe they are only worthwhile when they are acting in a worthwhile manner, they still will have a tendency to be mildly anxious due to the possibility that they no longer will earn the right to think highly of themselves. Children who hold the irrational idea that they can think highly of themselves only when they score in the top 10% of the class will experience anxiety due to the threat of falling out of this upper echelon. Every new test or assignment will be viewed as a threat to their ego. This nagging anxiety never will disappear entirely and will persist even when things are going beautifully.

What happens when these children do not succeed? How will they feel when they fail to make the honor roll or the baseball team? If children believe they are supposed to feel proud of themselves only when they succeed, most also will believe they should castigate and berate themselves when then fail. That is the way the self-esteem teeter-totter works. These irrational ideas regarding self-esteem have set kids up to be miserable.

Another problem with the currently popular view of self-esteem is that it stems from the contention that when children succeed, which is enjoyable, they should feel good about themselves. When they win first place in the spelling championship (which is enjoyable), they are supposed to feel good about themselves. But there is an error in this logic. Simply because a child was fortunate enough to experience something enjoyable does not mean he/she *should* feel good about himself/herself.

If children enjoy eating pizza and had the chance to eat their favorite kind of pizza, they would not feel proud of themselves. Conversely, they would not feel badly about themselves if they did not get to eat pizza. This seems to be the message in the misconceived ideas about self-esteem. If children succeed or accomplish something important, which is enjoyable, they can feel good about themselves. If they fail or do not reach their goals, they should feel like losers. Yet children's accomplishments are not a reflection of their value; accomplishments are just a measure of their performance in a given area. Academic grades, good or bad, cannot make kids any more or less worthwhile, but thousands of students' self-esteem depends upon their report cards. Grades are important, but not that important. As Ellis has stated, *a belief remains rational so long as it does not extend beyond the event or situation to the person's character.*

Some may believe that REBT states children are supposed to feel good about whatever traits they exhibit whether they display dishonesty, laziness, or other undesirable characteristics. REBT supports the evaluation of individual traits and behavior. There are obviously some traits, such as dishonesty, that most people dislike and even deplore. There are behaviors, like unprovoked violence, that are wrong and do not deserve to be condoned. But it is irrational to overgeneralize from the evaluation of an individual trait or specific behavior to the child's value as a person.

SYMPTOMS OF DEPRESSION

Depression, as mentioned in the beginning of this chapter, is an ever increasing problem. The following is a list of typical warning signs for depression.

- irritability
- feelings of hopelessness and worthlessness
- references to suicide (i.c., "I'd be better off dead." "Nobody would care if I wasn't around.")
- loss of energy
- change in sleep patterns, either waking up early and not being able to get back to sleep or wanting to sleep all the time
- significant change in weight
- loss of interest in sex
- giving away prized possessions
- interest in death (i.e., reading books or poetry on death)
- decrease in physical activity
- uncontrollable crying
- excessive guilt
- loss of interest in activities that were previously pleasurable

An important point to note is that a significant number of younger children do not present such classic symptoms as are listed here. Young children may not appear to be sad at all, which is why they often are misdiagnosed or go completely undiagnosed. The most common behavioral manifestation of depression in some children is anger. These clients cover their feelings of worthlessness with rage and often aggressively act out their anger. They often can be found in the principal's office because they are constantly in some sort of problem due to fights or difficulties getting along with peers. To assume these clients have conduct problems is easy because they do, but they also may be depressed.

There is still another substratum of depressed clients who may not even exhibit the above mentioned unmodulated hostility. It is not that these children are not angry, it is just that they are not as comfortable expressing their anger and frustration. They exhibit other behaviors that are negative predictors of adjustment such as the following:

- cruelty to animals,
- pyromania, and/or
- encopresis.

This small cluster of behaviors is indicative of other serious disorders, but be aware that many of these clients also are depressed and certainly have low self-esteem/acceptance.

ETIOLOGY OF DEPRESSION

Cognitive therapist Aaron Beck postulated three primary beliefs that lead to depression. Beck and Shaw (1977) referred to these beliefs as the cognitive triad.

1. Negative View of the Self

Another classic quotation from Ellis pertains to the negative thoughts that many depressed clients have regarding themselves. Ellis has stated that "all roads lead to s_ _ _hood" as a way of reminding counselors that most problems start with the core idea that "I am no good. I'm worthless. I'm lower than low." Typical self-talk from depressed clients who share this personal philosophy includes the following:

"I am no damn good and I never will amount to anything."
"I deserve the rotten treatment I get."
"No matter what I do I will fail."
"I can't do anything right."
"Nobody could love me because I am worthless."

How could a child feel anything but depressed if he/she walked around with these messages inside his/her head all day long? These messages play like a cassette tape, reinforcing the basic belief that "I am no damn good" until the tape becomes a part of the child's identity. Refer back to the discussion of cognitive dissonance and know that when students believe they are worthless, they will act as if that belief were an observable, scientific fact.

Another interesting phenomenon associated with children who suffer from these irrational beliefs is that they have a tendency to blame themselves excessively and to take responsibility for failures that were not their fault. The team on which they play loses, and they think ridiculous thoughts such as, "It's probably my fault because I was on the team. If only I had hit a home run every time up to bat we might have won."

What is more interesting is that when they do succeed, they often feel they deserve none of the credit. Depressed clients give away the recognition for their hard work and claim they were lucky or that they did not deserve to do well. This type of irrational thinking is emotional double jeopardy. If they fail a test, they think, "This proves how dumb I am." If they receive a high score, they think, "Boy, was I ever lucky."

2. Negative View of the World

Not only do depressed students feel *they* are hopeless, but many feel the *world* is hopeless as well. They seem to think the problems of the world are beyond repair.

"What's the point of going on?"
"You have to watch your back because people are out to take advantage of you."
"Any day now, the world is going to end. It can't go on like this."

To turn on a television without being bombarded with a host of brutal stories is nearly impossible. Children are especially susceptible to the type of reactive depression bad news can bring. Children lack the emotional toughness most adults have acquired after years of living. Children lose sight of the fact that while there are many things that occur in the world that most would describe as "bad," there also are many things most would find "good."

3. Negative View of the Future

Children who believe that the unfortunate circumstances they currently are experiencing will continue forever are also at risk of becoming depressed. Many look into the future and see nothing but darkness and more difficulties.

"There is no way out."
"I'll never get over this."
"I can't change the horrible things that have happened to me in the past, so I'm doomed forever."
"Life sucks now and will always suck."

An important point to realize is that there are many corollaries from the three core irrational beliefs contained in Beck's cognitive triad. Numerous variations exist, but all seem to have originated from one of these three. The sample self-messages printed above are just a few of the irrational beliefs that cluster around these core cognitions leading to depression.

What about clinical depression? Can "talking therapy" do anything to relieve symptoms related to biochemical imbalances in the brain? Research suggests that it can. A longitudinal study conducted in 1985 by the National Institute for Mental Health (Trimpey, 1992) found that *cognitive-behavioral approaches can be at least as effective as drug therapy in the treatment of depression.* Also, Rush, Beck, Kovacs, and Hollon (1977) found cognitive therapy to be *more* effective than antidepressant medication for treatment of the depressive syndrome.

This finding would appear to contradict a commonly held belief among some mental health professionals who believe drug therapy is the only treatment for clinical depression. A combination of psychotherapy and medication is certainly appropriate. Drug therapy can be used as a short-term solution designed to stabilize clients. Pharmacological intervention can be viewed as a means of buying time until the irrational beliefs at the root of most depression can be disputed and replaced. Clients can learn how they have caused or contributed to their depression and what things they can do to help themselves out of their malaise.

It is not only possible, but plausible, that the type of negative messages depressed clients send themselves affects the neurochemical functioning of their brains. If clients can think themselves out of depression, which research and clinician observations suggest they can, it is logical to believe that clients can think themselves into depression. The therapist's job is to help clients analyze the thoughts that sabotage their lives because *the beliefs they hold about themselves have as much, if not more, to do with their day-to-day functioning than any other variable.*

The real secret is not in getting kids to merely *feel* better, because almost any adult can help improve a child's mood simply by giving the kid a little time and attention. The real challenge lies in helping clients *think* better.

Chapter 14

DISPUTATIONS
AND INTERVENTIONS
WITH CLIENTS SUFFERING
FROM LOW SELF-ESTEEM
AND DEPRESSION

The following are cognitive, behavioral, and emotive disputations and techniques to be used with clients who have depression/self-esteem problems. Many of these techniques have been examined earlier in the book and only will be highlighted in this chapter.

COGNITIVE TECHNIQUES

One of the goals of most cognitive techniques is to get clients to question the logic of their beliefs (Walen et al., 1980).

Why Questions

Most schools of psychotherapy discourage "why" questions, but such questions can be used effectively in REBT.

Ben: *I'll never be able to be happy unless I find out who my dad is.*

Therapist: *Why won't you be able to be happy?*

B: *Because I've got to know.*

T: *I know you would like to know and I can certainly understand that, but why do you have to know?*

B: *I just really want to know.*

T: *There you go; now you've changed your statement to a prefer-ence, and we can deal with that. "I just really want to know" is a preference. When you have a preference and you're disappointed you feel bad, but when you've got a demand that doesn't go your way you feel like it's the worst thing in the world.*

Use of Humor

Even in cases of depression, humor can be used to help clients understand that their thinking is not making sense. It allows the therapist to demonstrate his/her concern and support for the client, but at the same time humor can be used to keep things in perspective.

Be careful that clients understand that you are not making fun of their situations. The intent is to get clients to realize their thinking is causing them trouble.

Therapist: *What are you saying to yourself about yourself?*

Holly: *That I'm good for nothing.*

T: *Do you really think you are not good for anything?*

H: *Yes. That's what my mom and dad tell me.*

T: *I bet I can find plenty of uses for you right here in my office. Stand up.* (Author's Note: I preceded to use Holly as a doorstop, pa-perweight, and tape holder. This nonsensical behavior provided me with the opportunity to make an important point.)

H: *So you want me to stand here all day and keep the door from hitting the wall?*

T: *No that would be really boring. I'm just trying to get you to think about what you said. You said you were absolutely good for nothing, and I showed you three things you were good for right here. I just want you to think about the truth of what you're thinking about yourself.*

By exaggerating the situation to such a ridiculous extreme it was hoped that the client would see that her thinking was irrational.

Challenging the "A"

Occasionally I will use a technique that is called challenging the "A," which is a means of examining the accuracy of the client's perceptions of the event (i.e., the "A"). An overweight client had an "A" that she was 10 pounds overweight. I went to the school nurse and got the chart that compares height with weight and found that the client was at the upper end of the average range. Her "A" was incorrect. She was not overweight at all but average for her height.

This approach is what Ellis has referred to as *inelegant* in that it does not attack the belief, causing the girl to have low self acceptance. She was thinking at point "B," "Because I'm overweight it proves what a rotten person I am." It is usually advisable to go after the "B," which is causing the upset emotion at point "C," but in certain circumstances, it is appropriate to challenge the "A."

Paradoxical Intention

The idea behind *paradoxical intention* is to persuade the client to behave paradoxically regarding the agreed-upon goals of treatment. For example, if a student is extremely depressed, try to convince the client to act as upbeat as possible. These techniques may be beneficial with clients who do not respond to other disputations. Ellis (1977a) stated that by behaving deliberately in a paradoxical manner, the client may feel less depressed.

There are other techniques that incorporate paradoxical features that can be beneficial. A variation of this approach is to give the client permission to be depressed but only for short periods of time. ("Try to be depressed only during recess.") If students are able to follow these directions, the amount of time they spend feeling upset is reduced significantly.

Cognitive Distraction

Another technique that I use primarily with resistant clients is *cognitive distraction*. This technique has the limitation of not challenging the student's philosophical beliefs about himself/herself, which are at the root of his/her feelings of low self-worth. As the name implies, this technique is merely a distraction designed to keep the client occupied with other thoughts.

An excellent cognitive distraction involves having a client think of either the funniest or happiest memory he/she has. The memory is best if it can bring an instantaneous smile or laugh to a client. Do not be surprised if it takes clients some time to think of an image or memory that will help. Some depressed clients will tell you, "I have no happy or funny memories." They may need some encouragement to come up with an appropriate image.

Instruct clients that when they are starting to feel themselves becoming depressed, they are to immediately picture their preselected scene. Some clients who do not respond well to other interventions are quite successful with this technique.

Cognitive distraction can be used as a means of buying time until clients are able to learn how they are upsetting themselves. It can help break the cycle of excessive rumination on the negative aspects of clients' situations.

BEHAVIORAL TECHNIQUES

Reinforcement

REBT encourages the use of standard behavioral techniques as the "B" in REBT implies. The most effective and commonly used behavioral intervention is *reinforcement* (rewards).

Rewards can be administered by parents after clients have completed the out-of-counseling exercises that are an important part of therapy. This type of program has the advantage of keeping the parents involved and aware of clients' treatment goals and progress.

Below is a list of commonly used reinforcers:

phone privileges
longer curfew

pizza
reduced chores
candy
Nintendo rental
camping
cassette
playing outside
no baby-sitting
movies
video rental
use of car
soft drinks
later bedtime
a special toy
special trip
staying over night
special time with parents
new clothes
money

Parents and clients have to work out an agreement with which both sides feel comfortable regarding rewards that can be earned.

Rubber Band Technique

A technique that is a distraction but is more behaviorally oriented is the rubber band technique. Clients are to wear rubber bands around their wrists. When they feel themselves using self-downing thinking, they are to snap themselves with the rubber band. The snapping of the rubber band is a reminder to practice their rational beliefs and rational coping statements immediately.

This technique also can be used when clients hear themselves thinking, "I'm a no good slob," "The future is hopeless," etc. When they catch themselves thinking such IBs, they are to snap themselves and replace these irrational beliefs with rational thoughts.

The snapping is a mildly aversive stimulus, but it would be incorrect to think of this technique as punishment. The snapping is more helpful as a reminder for clients to use their rational coping statements.

Stop Ruminating

Depressed clients have a tendency to wallow in their misery. They start to feel down and zero in on their feelings of hopelessness. Pretty soon they have spiraled into a deep depression.

Counselors have to convince depressed clients to have a plan to stop this cycle of rumination. It does not matter what they do as long as they do something to break the cycle of "stinking thinking." Counselors can help clients with this plan and add suggestions if clients cannot come up with any spontaneously.

A usually advisable procedure is for clients to get out of the house if that is possible. Intense physical exercise is great at breaking this cycle because endorphins are released by exercising. If a client is athletic, a counselor can have the client sign a contract or at least verbally agree that the client will go for a run or walk if he/she finds himself/herself slipping into this cycle of negative thinking.

EMOTIVE TECHNIQUES

Rational Emotive Imagery (REI)

REI must be used only with great care with depressed clients. The goal of REI is to get the client to picture the upsetting event as vividly as possible. Instead of feeling very depressed about the situation, the client is to feel only mildly upset. The problem I have had is that while the client is reexamining the "A" (a boyfriend/girlfriend leaving), he/she becomes very emotional and is unable to do the second half of this exercise effectively (calming himself/herself down from depression to sadness). I prefer REI with clients who have anger and anxiety problems as opposed to depression.

Forceful Dialogue

This disputation encourages clients to argue forcefully with themselves regarding their irrational beliefs. This technique resembles a conversation except that there is only one person talking. The client is speaking both the rational and irrational voices.

When clients are first learning to use this technique, I recommend that they actually speak out loud to themselves. After they have become proficient at forceful dialogue, they can do this disputing in their heads.

Irrational: *I'm never going to find someone to love me.*

Rational: *That may be true, but there is no way of knowing that at this point. Nobody knows the future, but even if there were nobody to love me I probably could still manage to be at least a little happy in my life.*

Irrational: *The world is too messed up to continue.*

Rational: *The world always has had its problems and yet we're still here. The best bet is we'll be here for a long time to come.*

This technique can be used with the client during therapy sessions. Therapist and client can take turns being the rational and irrational voices. This is similar to another emotive technique called rational role reversal (RRR).

Full Acceptance

The intervention of full acceptance is a philosophical approach as much as it is an intervention or disputation. By full acceptance it is meant that the therapist fully accepts the client with all of his/her positive *and* negative traits. This does not mean that the therapist accepts any and all *behavior* from the client. As discussed earlier, clients are accepted as people, but it is understood that their behavior can be deplorable.

The fact that clients have problem areas in their lives does not make them rotten people. Clients who suffer from low self-acceptance often make this type of overgeneralization. They mistakenly believe that because they are less than perfect, they are worthless. If the counselor demonstrates to clients that he/she accepts them (and their problems), the hope is that the clients will be able to accept themselves.

The above is presented as an ideal, and like most ideals, in reality people can fall short. There are some clients who are difficult to work with and difficult to like. For the counselor to share his/her feelings about the client's behavior in a direct but nonpejorative manner is appropriate at times. This also can be very effective when carried out in a group situation by the client's peers.

Flat Tire Technique

Howard Young (1977) used a technique I call *flat tire* to get clients to stop overgeneralizing, which is at the core of most self-acceptance problems.

> **Therapist:** *Alissa, if you had a brand new car and it was just perfect, you'd treat it nicely, wouldn't you?*
>
> **Alissa:** *What do you mean?*
>
> **T:** *I mean you would make sure it was clean and shiny.*
>
> **A:** *Sure.*
>
> **T:** *If that brand new car had a problem like a flat tire, you wouldn't throw the car out, would you?*
>
> **A:** *If it was brand new? No way. I'd try to fix it.*
>
> **T:** *Of course you would; you wouldn't throw it on the junk heap because there was still a lot of cool stuff about that car. But you know what, when you get so down on yourself for making a mistake, you're taking yourself and throwing yourself right on the junk pile. Instead of fixing the flat tire, trying to do a better job of getting along with your little brother, you're throwing yourself on the junk pile. What do you think about that?*
>
> **A:** *That's crazy.*

Rational Role Reversal (RRR)

RRR is a technique that could be included in the cognitive section of this chapter but is categorized as emotive because it helps deepen a client's conviction to rational thinking. There is some interesting research on the phenomenon of cognitive dissonance to support the concept behind RRR.

RRR involves the client and therapist switching roles. The therapist tells the client what made the client feel depressed, and the client's job is to dispute the irrational ideas put forth by the therapist. This technique is usually fun for both the client and therapist but also provides the therapist with valuable information regarding which ideas the client has comprehended fully. Particular attention should be paid to the disputations clients choose because these are the arguments that have made the biggest impression on clients.

Assertiveness Training

Helping students learn to stand up for themselves is included as an intervention because many times low self-acceptance is associated with shyness or a lack of assertiveness. When students are able to assert themselves in an appropriate manner, they are less likely to be taken advantage of and hopefully will experience less self-downing.

One of the most effective means of teaching students to be more assertive is through *role-play* or *behavioral rehearsal*. Students are encouraged to give examples of situations where they find it difficult to stand up for themselves. Once they have given the therapist or group a couple of examples of how they fail to stand up for themselves, they can be given the opportunity to practice being assertive in similar situations. The therapist or group can give each student feedback on his/her performance, and the individual can role-play the situation again.

When this assignment is especially difficult for some clients, it is be a good idea to examine the irrational beliefs causing them difficulties and keeping them from being more assertive. My experience has been that the core irrational belief associated with a lack of assertiveness usually contains a rational and irrational segment. Students usually believe, "If I told them what I really thought or felt, they may not like me," which is rational. People will tell others that they respect them for being able to stand up for what they believe, but a good many will dislike their assertiveness.

The irrational belief associated with a lack of assertiveness is usually, "And if they didn't like me, that would be *horrible* or prove what a *rotten person* I am." This irrational belief then can be disputed and, hopefully, the student will come to realize that if others did not like him/her, it would not be a catastrophe. Nobody ever died from another's dislike, or certainly we all would be dead. Another's dislike would not prove what a rotten person the client is because another person's opinion has no real power over anyone else.

Rational Story Telling Technique (RSTT)

The RSTT technique was described earlier in the chapter on anger disputations (Chapter 8). A 7-year-old, Tim, told me the following story.

Tim: *Once upon a time, there was an old man who lived in the woods. He lived all alone and nobody ever came to his house to play. The old man was very sad because he wanted to have lots of friends but nobody liked him.*

Therapist: *My story is also about an old man who lived in the woods. He also wanted to have friends but didn't have very many. He thought about it and decided even if most other people who lived in the woods didn't like him that didn't mean he couldn't try to be happy anyway. At least he could try to be their friend and hope that they would learn to like him. If they didn't, he wasn't going to get mad about it or think he was a bad old man because he knew in his heart he was a good person. So he tried to be nice to others and the other people in the woods took their time before they liked him. They remembered the times he had been mean to them so it took quite a while. The old man was happy that he learned how to like himself first, and that made it easier for others to like him.*

Chapter 15

TRANSCRIPTS FROM A DEPRESSED CLIENT'S SESSION

What follows is a session with an 18-year-old male, Dan, who was referred to me by the courts due to a suicide attempt. He had been seeing a girl, who we will call Wendy, off and on for nearly three years when things fell apart and Dan contemplated suicide.

Therapist: *Tell me what happened the night you tried to kill yourself.*

Dan: *I didn't try to kill myself, but I was thinking about it.*

T: *The person who set this up told me it was court ordered. How did the courts get involved?*

D: *I had a gun and told someone I was thinking about killing myself, and they called the police.*

T: *Tell me about that night.*

D: *I had this girlfriend, and she and I have been dating off and on for almost three years. Sometimes it's great, but we have broken up twice before. She moved in with this other guy for a while after we broke up the first time, but then things didn't work out with him so she came back to me. Then last summer she broke up with me again.*

137

T: *Sounds like you guys have a pretty rocky relationship.*

D: *Yeah, we do. I tried to get her back again, and we had been dating, but it wasn't like before.*

T: *What do you mean it wasn't like before?*

D: *We weren't just dating each other. Well, I wasn't seeing anybody, but she was dating a couple of other guys.*

T: *Which pissed you off to no end.*

D: *Yeah. That about drove me crazy. The night all this happened I asked her out the week before and decided I was going to try to get her back for just me again. I bought her flowers and the whole bit. We went out to a really nice restaurant and everything. Then I told her I wanted her back, and she said she didn't think it would work out.*

T: *And you thought what?*

D: *I don't know exactly but I was . . .*

T: *See if you can think back to that night. When did you decide that killing yourself might not be a bad idea?*

D: *After dinner we went back to her place and fought for about an hour or two. I don't know how long it was, but it was a long time.*

T: *And when did you decide to, or think about killing yourself?*

D: *On the way home.*

T: *Did you have a plan?*

D: *Yeah. I knew where the gun was in the house, and my folks were out for the evening. I was just crying and hitting things.*

T: *Let me ask you something. Was part of this sort of a "I'll show her. They'll really miss me when I'm gone"?*

D: *Yeah, but not too much. I just felt like my life was nothing without her.* (Author's Note: This statement ["My life was nothing without her"] was very important and was probably at the core of the depression and suicidal ideation.)

T: *One of the things I want to do, Dan, is check out how you are feeling right now. If you had to rate how you are feeling on a scale between 1 and 100, with 1 being very bad and 100 being very good, where would you rate yourself?*

D: *Right now.*

T: *Today.*

D: *Probably about . . . 40.*

T: *40. Where were you on this scale the night you thought about killing yourself?*

D: *About a 1.*

T: *So things have improved quite a bit.*

D: *Yeah.*

T: *Are you thinking about hurting yourself now?*

D: *No, not really.*

T: *What do you mean not really?*

D: *No I'm not. I feel pretty bad, but I'm not going to do anything like that.*

T: *Will you make me an absolute promise?*

D: *Yes.*

T: *Cross your heart?*

D: (laughs) *Cross my heart.*

T: *Good. I want you to know that most suicidal impulses can come on very fast, and even though things can seem OK, one little thing can* *trigger stuff like that. I'm in the phone book, and you know how to get a hold of me during the day. You'll call me if you get any ideas about hurting yourself?*

D: *Yeah.*

T: *What I'm still confused about is how the police, was it the police that found out about this?*

D: *It was the police. I called Wendy and told her what I was going to do, and she called the police.*

T: *And they came and did what?*

D: *They took me to Lakeland.*

T: *What was that like?*

D: *I hated that place. I was there for two days and three nights. People in that place are really . . . nuts. One guy down the hall just wouldn't shut up, and this other girl just sat in the corner all day and . . . Uh, I'm really glad to be away from that place.*

T: *Yeah, I don't blame you. Let me explain a little bit about the way we're going to work together. I use a system of therapy that I'm going to teach you. I've played around with a lot of these, and the one I'm going to teach you is by far the best one I've ever used. I can tell from talking with you that you're bright, and that's always good.*

The way this system works is to examine the kinds of thoughts you have and help you decide if these thoughts make sense. I like to think that we're on a search for the truth. We're going to try to decide if what you are telling yourself is true or false or, as I like to call it, rational or irrational.

Now, I'm going to tell you . . . well, let me ask you something first. What do you think caused you to feel so bad the night you thought about hurting yourself?

D: *Wendy deciding she didn't want to be with me.*

T: *That's what almost every single man, woman, and child would think, and I'm not at all surprised that you think that. But you know what? That's not true. It's actually something else.* (Author's Note: Clients usually look at the therapist like he/she is completely insane at this point, but that is to be expected. The therapist is presenting information that is the antithesis of what the general public believes.)

D: *I guess I don't follow you.*

T: *People think that feelings like you were having are caused by things that happen to us, like Wendy telling you she didn't want to be your girlfriend. But actually it's what you are thinking about what she told you. Let me see if I can give you an example to help. If Wendy's not wanting to be your girlfriend made you feel a certain way, then she must have some magical power in those words that could affect other people. But what if she told the exact same thing to, let's say, your grandma?*

D: (laughing) *My grandma probably would think that was pretty weird.*

T: *Exactly. Would your grandma feel as bad as you felt?*

D: *No, because she doesn't love Wendy.*

T: *Right, but the words would be exactly the same. So if it isn't the words, it must be something else. It must be what you thought about the words. What did you say to yourself, actually you said it earlier. You said, "I felt like my life was nothing without her."*

D: *I still feel like that.*

T: *And it's that exact belief that is causing you to feel so depressed today. Once you give up that idea you'll still feel a sense of loss, but you won't feel so hopeless.*

D: *I don't know how to do that.*

T: *That's my job to help you. We'll have some hard work together, but I'll make you a promise. If you do what I ask of you, you'll feel better. You won't feel great over night, but you'll feel better. I've worked with lots of folks with problems like yours, and I think I can help you, too.* (Author's Note: I say things like this not to be arrogant but to give the client a sense of faith in my skills. It's important to try to be as positive as possible but still make certain the client understands there will be a lot of work ahead.)

T: *Remember a while ago I said we were going to try to look at what you tell yourself and decide if it was true or false, or rational or irrational, as I like to call it? One of the easiest ways to try to do that is to look at a belief and see if there is any proof for that belief. If there is proof, we know a belief is rational, and if we can't find proof, it is irrational. Now let's look at the belief you said earlier, "My life is nothing without her." Can we prove that belief to be true?*

D: *What do you mean?*

T: *Is there any proof for that belief? Any evidence?*

D: *No, not really.*

T: *Is that belief helping you or hurting you?*

D: *Probably making me feel worse, isn't it?*

T: *I think so. Is it making your life easier or harder?*

D: *Probably harder.*

T: *You're going to be good at this, I can tell that already. Let's work on a thought you can use when you find yourself thinking, "My life will be nothing without her." How can you change that so it is a true or rational belief?*

D: *Maybe I could think about the good times we had.*

T: *OK, but right now let's work on something to replace that belief that "My life will be nothing without her." It's important to get that out of your head because that's one of the thoughts that's messing you up right now. There are probably a few more in there, but let's work on that one right now.*

D: *I could think I won't be stupid enough to take her back.*

T: *Let me see if I can help you out. Try to change the old belief by just a word or two.*

D: *Like, "My life will be OK even without her."*

T: *That's fine. Now let's ask some questions to determine if that one is rational. Will that belief make your life easier or harder?*

D: *I won't feel as bad, I don't think.*

T: *Right. Will it help you feel the kinds of feelings you want to feel?*

D: *I'm not sure; I've never thought that before.*

T: *What's your best guess?*

D: *I don't know, because I'd still probably take her back if she'd come back. I guess it would help me feel less bummed out, less desperate about things.*

T: *That's what I would guess, too. Let me write that one down for you. OK, I want to go over one more thing with you before you go. We'll see each other next Wednesday, but until then I want you to know there might be times when you start thinking about Wendy and then you may start feeling really down. If that happens, I don't want you to sit around and stew about what has happened. OK?*

D: *OK.*

T: *If that happens, what are some things you could do other than sit around and feel bad?*

D: *I could call a friend.*

T: *Good, what else?*

D: *I like to lift weights. Go for a drive or something I guess.*

T: *Both of those are fine. The important thing is that you get out of that mood by doing something to occupy yourself. Do you understand why?*

D: *Because you just sit around feeling sorry for yourself and feel even worse.*

T: *That's right. All right, we're going to get together next Wednesday. Do you have any other questions right now?*

D: *I'm not sure I really believe that my life will be OK without her. We've been together for so long and I love her even though she doesn't treat me very well.*

T: *I understand that, because you've been thinking, "Without Wendy my life is empty and meaningless," right? That tape has been playing in your head for quite a while, hasn't it?*

D: *Yeah. Like I said, we've been together for almost three and a half years.*

T: *You've got a habit of thinking that way, and habits can be hard to break, but I really think I can help you think clearer about this. You've probably broken habits before. I bet you used to suck your thumb when you were little, but you don't do that anymore.*

D: *That's different.*

T: *I know. That's probably not a good example, but I'm just trying to show you that you can learn to change the way you think if you're really tired of this merry-go-round.*

D: *Well, I am sick of the way she treats me, and I think I've finally learned she's not going to change. But I said that last time. I really think I mean it this time though.*

T: *It's hard to make yourself believe that the person you care about doesn't really care about you or at least doesn't care about you the way you would like her to. But you know what? We can't change her. We've got absolutely no control over her, but you've got a lot of control over how you react to what she does. That's what we're going to focus on. OK?*

D: *OK.*

PART F
GROUP WORK

Chapter 16

REBT GROUPS FOR LOW SELF-ESTEEM, DEPRESSION, AND ANXIETY

What follows is a curriculum for a group counseling program to be used with students who are struggling with issues such as low self-esteem, depression, and anxiety. In the high school where I work, these assemblages are known as "Rational Thinking Groups" and draw a very diverse crowd. A separate chapter (Chapter 17) focusing on the use of REBT concepts in anger control groups will follow.

Some may be wondering why the book contains a separate chapter for anger control groups yet combines depression and anxiety. The length of the book was one consideration, but there were other considerations that will be addressed briefly.

The types of clients attending anger control (AC) groups are very different from clients who participate in general REBT groups that focus on self-esteem, anxiety, and other issues. AC groups usually are heavily populated with males, and these males' perceptions, attitudes, and beliefs tend to be very different from general REBT clients. Clients in AC groups believe the world *has* to be the way they would like it to be, whereas clients in the other groups do not possess such demanding (dare I say grandiose) ideas.

My primary reason for combining depression and anxiety has to do with the overlap between the two in regards to the group plans. Many of the initial activities in early weeks of group are virtually identical. Later on, the activities used in group are similar, and the only difference is in the application of techniques.

During the first week of REBT group, ask the members, "Why are your here? What do you want to get out of this experience?" In some instances there will be a dominant theme such as self-esteem, but it is not uncommon for students to be interested in learning more about rational thinking. Often students would like to understand how their thoughts influence, and largely determine, their emotions.

As our culture continues to unravel, schools are being asked to be more involved with the socialization of children. Usually the kinds of socialization activities that go on in classrooms will suffice, but for an ever increasing number of students, more structured interventions may be necessary.

Children are being forced to live in homes where substance abuse, domestic violence, and various other deleterious situations exist. All of the above mentioned factors interfere with the child's ability to focus on school. *Students cannot turn off their lives outside of the classroom simply because the teacher would like to give a spelling test.* Educational support groups have become one means through which children's noneducational needs can be met. That is why group counseling in schools has become so popular. Since schools have to do more with less, groups are a means of trying to meet those needs.

ORGANIZATION

Group Sign-up

While the faculty is one source for referrals to the REBT group, it is also important to allow students to refer themselves. Posters and flyers can be placed around the school with information about groups that will be starting. These posters and flyers can contain the name of an individual or individuals to contact if students would like more information about the group.

A more effective way to recruit members is through short classroom presentations. This can be accomplished by going directly into classes and briefly explaining the various groups offered. Each student is to receive a sign-up sheet during the presentations to avoid the stigma that can occur when only a handful of students return sign-up slips to the front of the room. If every student has a sheet, no one will know who is or is not interested in signing up for the groups. Some students will not care if others know they are interested, but others might be discouraged from signing up if they will be identified. Their right to privacy can be protected easily by following the simple procedure described above.

After the sign-up sheets are received back from the numerous classroom presentations, various members of the guidance/psychologist/social worker departments screen the students individually to explain the goals of the group, meeting time, location, and general expectations. Students can decide if the group is something they would like to explore or if they may not be interested. At this time, students should be asked to read and sign a contract. (A sample contract is provided in Figure 1.) If students are not sure, it is best to let them attend the sessions for a couple of weeks to determine if they would like to keep meeting with the group. If they want to leave the group after giving the program a trial, no pressure should be exerted for them to stay.

SAMPLE CONTRACT

I hereby agree to the below stated terms of this contract. I am signing this contract under my own free will and pledge to honor these commitments.

1. I will be on time for all group meetings.

2. I will make up any and all missed assignments due to group participation.

3. I am willing to change my attitudes and behavior. I do not expect the entire world to change for me.

4. I will complete all practice exercises from the group to the best of my ability.

5. I will be a supportive member of the group and try to help other members.

Name

Date

Figure 1.   Sample contract for group participants.

Information about the groups also is sent home in student handbooks. By having information in student handbooks, parents who would like to refer their child know whom to contact.

Size of Group

The size of a group is an important decision that needs to be addressed. There are real advantages to having manageable numbers such as four to six students, but that is not always possible or practical. If you run groups with only four students you may be trying to conduct more support groups than your schedule permits. A general recommendation of eight students per group is a good rule. An absolute maximum is 10 students per group. When numbers exceed 10, a point is reached where the needs of students no longer are being met. Group members feel cheated because there is not enough time to let them discuss their issues.

Time Span

The length of a group also needs to be taken into consideration. REBT is very much a "teaching" therapy, and groups tend to resemble small classrooms. Six to eight weeks is usually sufficient time to cover the content necessary in REBT groups. This is not a hard and fast rule but merely a suggestion. It might be advisable to schedule a follow-up meeting in two weeks or a month to check on the progress of the group members.

MANAGEMENT TECHNIQUES

As in any situation with children, managing the behavior of the partici-pants in these groups has to be considered in order to maximize the group's efforts. Below are a few techniques to help manage the behavior of unruly group members.

Speaking Ball

A ball is passed around the group. The only individual with permission to speak is the person holding the ball. The group leader(s) has (have) the right to speak with or without the ball. While this technique may seem childish and only appropriate with younger children, the "speaking ball" can be used with older students.

Divide and Conquer

When cofacilitating a group, do not hesitate to divide the group into two smaller groups. Some activities work better this way because students have more time to speak. Smaller numbers allow facilitators to keep better control over students. Dividing the group also allows cofacilitators to separate two group members who are not working well together.

Time-out

Educators and parents are hopefully familiar with the use of "time-out." This technique can be used in support groups to improve behavior. When members are acting inappropriately, ask those individuals to leave the group for a time-out. This usually happens only once, and the rest of the group members settle down.

Reserve the right to send a student back to class or to the office if he/she continues to act up. If a group member's behavior is interfering with the goals of the group, he/she can be removed permanently.

Cofacilitation

Another consideration is whether to run the groups alone or cofacilitate. There are both advantages and disadvantages to having a cofacilitator. There may be less problems controlling the students' behavior with two adults in the room. Another adult also is able to help with the organization of the group (i.e., writing passes, making photocopies, etc.).

After recently completing an REBT group at the high school where I work, my cofacilitator was telling some of her colleagues about the group and how much she had learned from the experience. Other teachers had an interest in the information presented in the group. This interest lead to an REBT group for teachers to deal with issues such as stress, anger, and other dilemmas facing educators. The teachers group was so successful that another group will be offered in the fall.

Having a cofacilitator has some potential problems as well. If cofacilitators do not agree on one another's approach, it probably would be unwise for them to run a group together. Conflicting ideas in the course of a group can lead to numerous other difficulties.

Use of Repeating Group Members

It might be advisable to take advantage of any group members who have been through this group or another support group prior to joining. These students are usually the leaders in the school who can be helpful by modeling appropriate problem-solving techniques. They can view themselves as "student helpers" or "peer helpers."

If this is your first attempt at this type of group, a helpful procedure is to meet with several students ("confederates") prior to group and teach them about REBT. An excellent resource is *A Rational Counseling Primer* (Young, 1974), which can be given to the peer helpers and also can be used in the group. These confederates need to have a good understanding of the ABCs as well as the most commonly occurring irrational ideas leading to depression and anxiety.

The potential benefits of using confederates in group are as follows:

1. They can model appropriate behavior in group.
2. They can be used to help clarify important points.
3. They can demonstrate appropriate problem-solving approaches.

WEEKLY ACTIVITIES

Week 1

The initial week of group usually requires a lot of "business" to be taken care of before the lessons can begin. In smaller districts, all of the kids know each other, but if some group members are not acquainted with other group members, introductions are in order. Students can state their names, grades, what they would like to be called in group, and what they are hoping to get out of group (i.e., their goals).

After introductions, hand out schedules for the following meetings. Any other group business, such as receiving a pass to come to group or the location of next week's meeting, can be covered at this time. This is also the time to establish group rules.

Rules can be handled in different ways, but it is important to have a few guidelines to keep the group running smoothly. Some sample rules are as follows:

1. Be on time.
2. What is said in group, stays in group (confidentiality).
3. No personal attacks or "slams."
4. One person speaks at a time.
5. Everyone has the right to "pass" or not participate in an activity.
6. Be honest and respectful.

The importance of confidentiality cannot be overemphasized. Take a few minutes to make certain students understand that being able to feel safe sharing personal information is extremely important. It is not a break in confidentiality for the students to share what *they* spoke about in group, but they must not share what other people said or mention the names of other group members. They can tell people in general terms what went on in group as long as they leave out specific details.

Rate Your Week.   An "icebreaker" activity I use to start every group is called "Rate Your Week." Students take turns giving their week a number between 1 and 10 and then explain why their week was a "6" or a "9." During the initial week of group, try to plan activities that require participation in order to let everyone hear his/her voice in the room. Some members will be anxious about speaking in front of other students. A few planned activities where everyone speaks is a good way to handle this anxiety.

Idea Inventory.   Before any lessons begin is a good time to pretest students with an instrument such as the *Idea Inventory* (Kassinove, Crisci, & Tiegerman, 1977). This is a short instrument that will allow you to chart the effectiveness of the group. In order to determine if students have improved during the course of group, it is necessary to use the *Idea Inventory* as a posttest to compare with their earlier results.

Lesson for the Week: Thoughts Cause Feelings.   Most people believe that events, not thoughts, cause feelings. While events have a definite impact on the emotions experienced, it is the thoughts, beliefs, and attitudes individuals carry that have a dominant role in determining the feelings they will experience.

The best way to illustrate this point is through using a group member's recent experience. Ask someone to give an example of when he/she made himself/herself upset. Record the "A" and the "C."

A—Got rejected for a date.
C—Angry, sad.

Explain that "A" did not cause "C." As much as it may seem that way, there is a middle part—"B"—that actually caused "C." Ask if it would be possible for someone to get rejected for a date and not be angry and sad. This is an excellent time to use your confederates if you have them. If none of the other group members are able to give you an example of a student being happy about being rejected, make one up. A student could be happy he/she were rejected because it would allow time to go out of town with friends for the weekend.

Usually students can come up with several different emotions other than anger and sadness that they might experience after being rejected. If students report different emotions (such as anxiety), explain that their feelings are different because their thoughts are different. A student could be sad that he/she were rejected for a date because the student had been looking forward to getting to know better the person whom was asked out. Anxiety could result from a student knowing that friends would tease him/her if they found out that he/she had been rejected.

Tell "The Blind Man on the Bus" story and perform an ABC analysis: While traveling on a bus, you feel a sharp poke in the ribs ("A"). Ask the students what they were thinking to themselves ("B") to feel angry ("C").

A—Got poked in the ribs.
B—"People shouldn't poke other people in the ribs."
C—Angry.

Then explain that the man who did the poking was blind and did not mean to hurt anybody. Because the man was blind, he could not see the person he poked and, therefore, the poke was unintentional. Perform an ABC analysis with this new information.

A—Got poked in the ribs.
B—"It was an accident. He didn't mean to poke me."
C—Not angry but possibly pity, ashamed, etc.

Many students will report that when they saw the man was blind not only were they no longer angry, but they now felt (1) pity for the man and/or (2) ashamed that they were angry to begin with.

Once this realization has been made, the important point can be made that events (getting poked in the ribs) are not completely responsible for emotions (anger, pity, shame). How could the same event at point "A" cause several different emotions at point "C"? Once students understand the implications of the blind man story, it is time to transfer this logic to the example given earlier or to another example such as getting referred to the office at school.

A—Got an office referral for being late to class.
B—"I shouldn't have gotten an office referral. It's not fair, and I have to be treated fairly."
C—Anger.

This probably will take up all the time available for Week 1. If you do not have sufficient time to teach these essential concepts in Week 1, come back to these points during Week 2. This outline is just a rough plan regarding order of presentation. Some weeks lessons flow smoothly, which leaves time remaining, and other weeks things take longer than anticipated. Do not hesitate to adapt the schedule to fit the needs of your group.

Homework. Hand out *A Rational Counseling Primer*, which can be purchased through the Institute for Rational-Emotive Therapy at (800) 323-IRET. The group's homework is to read the book and write a paragraph or two about the book's main idea. The group may grumble about homework being assigned, but if they plan on getting the most out of this experience, they are going to have to practice between sessions. Homework assignments are stated clearly in the group contract they signed.

Week 2

Start with "Rate Your Week" if you are going to use that exercise weekly. This activity allows the facilitators to "check in" with the group and also provides topics for discussion in the group.

At the start of Week 2, it is appropriate to review the rules of the group that were conceived during Week 1. This only takes a few minutes and will not need to be done again unless group members violate the rules.

Check on the homework from Week 1. Does everyone have a paragraph written about the book? Have students either read their paragraphs or describe what they thought was the main idea of the book. If there are missing assignments, why?

Lesson for the Week: Rational vs. Irrational. It is now time to help students learn to distinguish rational from irrational beliefs. With younger students, you may need to substitute "true" and "false" for rational and irrational.

Maultsby (1975) encouraged clients to ask the following questions to determine if a belief is rational:

1. Can I prove this belief to be true?
2. Does this belief help to protect my life and health?
3. Does this belief help me get what I want?
4. Does this thinking help me avoid unwanted conflicts with others?
5. Does this belief help me feel the emotions I want to feel?

If the answer is "yes" to any three of the five, the belief in question is rational or mostly rational. If two or less can be answered in the affirmative, the belief is irrational.

Emphasize the need for *proof* to substantiate that a belief as rational. The following story is a good method of teaching how proof is gathered: "Suppose someone invented a miracle pill and claimed that it would cause people to lose 10 pounds overnight. How would the public know whether that belief was true or false?"

Students often state that there could be an experiment in which the pill would be given to people (or animals) before they went to sleep at night. In the morning they could be weighed and if they lost 10 pounds, there would be proof that the pill works and the belief would be true. If they did not lose the weight, the belief would be false.

The same search for proof can help people determine if other beliefs are true or false. The worksheet, "Where's the Proof?" (Figure 2), can be completed in class. If students do not have sufficient time to finish the worksheet in group, their homework assignment should be to complete the worksheet and bring it to class for Week 3. If students finish the worksheet in class, a substitute homework assignment is to have students explain to a teacher or other adult how to determine if a belief is true or false. Group members also can quiz an adult using the worksheet they have just completed. (Answers for "Where's the Proof?" worksheet are as follows: 1T, 2F, 3T, 4F, 5T, 6F, 7F, 8F, 9F, 10T, 11F, 12F, 13F, 14T.)

Week 3

After "Rate Your Week" and checking on homework, go over the "Where's the Proof?" worksheet (Figure 2). Spend time disputing why some beliefs are true and some are false. Help students learn to watch for key words like *must,*

WHERE'S THE PROOF?

Name_____

Directions: In the blank space in front of each belief, make a "T" if the belief is a true belief and an "F" if the belief is a false belief.

_____ 1. I don't like it when I do poorly, but it's not the worst thing in the world.

_____ 2. Life has to be fair all the time.

_____ 3. If people don't like me, I still can like myself.

_____ 4. I can't stand losing at something important.

_____ 5. I wish things in school were easier, but they don't have to be.

_____ 6. Other people make me feel bad.

_____ 7. If I make a mistake once, I probably will always make that mistake.

_____ 8. Because math is hard for me, it proves I'm a stupid person.

_____ 9. If someone thinks I'm a nerd, I'm a nerd.

_____10. No matter what you say or do to me, I'm still a worthwhile person.

_____11. When things don't go the way I want, it's the worst thing ever.

_____12. I have to be right 100% of the time.

_____13. Things should go my way most of the time.

_____14. For the most part, I can control how I feel.

Figure 2. Where's the Proof? worksheet. Permission is granted to photocopy for classroom use.

should, always, etc. Pay particular attention to #6 ("Other people make me feel bad."). This is certain to bring about disagreement among group members.

Lesson for the Week: The ABCs of Emotion. The ABCs are an important part of REBT, and helping students understand this system is an essential step in helping students think rationally. There are a couple of ways to present the ABCs.

I recently discovered an excellent videotape entitled "Rational High School" that I now use to teach this portion of the group. It was written and produced by Dr. James Larsen while he was employed as a school psychologist for Milwaukee Public Schools. To receive information on the tape contact the following:

School Psychological Services
Milwaukee Public Schools
P.O. Box 10 - K
Milwaukee, WI 53201

Another method of teaching the ABCs is to ask the group to present a problem from the previous week that they would like to examine. If this is a "self-acceptance" group, hopefully the problem will be related to this issue. Conversely, if the group is focusing on "anxiety," it would be best for the group to try to use an example that fits with the goals of the group. Perhaps someone brought up a problem during "Rate Your Week" that was of interest. Refer back to the Chapter 4 on the ABCs of REBT for help in teaching this concept.

Eventually, group members can learn to perform an ABC analysis in their heads and do not need to write the steps down on paper. They can analyze their thoughts anywhere to determine how they are tripping themselves up and also can learn how to give up their irrational demands easily by changing only a few words that will turn an IB into an RB.

Homework.   Students are to perform an ABC analysis on their own. They can be provided with homemade ABC forms to help them remember the steps if necessary. Professionally designed forms are also available through the following:

Institute for Rational-Emotive Therapy
45 East 65th Street
New York, NY 10021

Week 4

Start with "Rate Your Week" and proceed to check on homework. It may take some time to analyze students' ABC analyses, but it is a good idea to give students' feedback as early as possible. My experience has been that it is difficult for students to learn the ABCs, and a good portion of Week 4 may be

spent on this topic as well. When you do get through with the homework, it is time to have some fun!

Lesson for the Week: "Let's Get Rational" Board Game. During Week 4, the "Let's Get Rational" (LGR) board game can be used. This game, which I invented in 1990, is a nice way to reinforce the basic concepts of REBT. By this point in group, students are tired of worksheets and practice. With LGR, they can have a change of pace but still practice their new thinking skills. LGR is a counseling board game that can be used with both groups and individuals. It is designed for clients aged 11 through adulthood, although students younger than 11 who are abstract thinkers can benefit from playing the game as well. Write or call the Institute for RET (45 East 65th Street, New York, NY 10021) (1-800-323-IRET) for information on obtaining a copy of "Let's Get Rational." You also can write to the following address:

Jerry Wilde
East Troy Elementary
P. O. Box 257
East Troy, WI 53120

The game is played like most standard board games. A die is rolled, and a player moves the required number of spaces and performs whatever action is requested depending upon the square on which he/she lands. Approximately one-half of the squares have directions designed to encourage self-disclosure:

- Tell the group about a conflict you had this week.
- Tell the person to your left one thing you've learned about him/her through this group.
- Tell the group what is most on your mind today.
- Tell the group what you would like to improve about yourself.

The four "Affirmation" squares have a special purpose. When a player lands on an affirmation square, the other players in the group take turns making a positive, affirming statement about the player. Finally, the player who landed on the affirmation square makes a self-affirming statement. Affirmation squares can have a dramatic effect on the group. The sharing of affirming statements can be an emotional experience and can draw the group closer together.

Two "Role-play" squares are included. These squares are designed to give players practice performing an action that is difficult for them. Some of the role-play cards focus on the ABC system that has been discussed previously. Sample role-play cards are as follows:

- Perform an ABC and D analysis of a situation where you find it easy to make yourself angry.
- Perform an ABC and D analysis of a situation where you find yourself putting yourself down because of your behavior.

Other role-play cards require group members to "act out" a situation:

- Role-play being assertive in a situation where it would be best to stand up for yourself.
- Role-play resolving a conflict with a friend or family member.

Ten squares are entitled "Rational Reminder Pickup Cards." When a player lands on one of these squares, he/she is to pick from the pile of rational reminder cards and read aloud what the card says. Some examples are as follows:

- Life does not have to be better or different because you want it to be that way. You either can accept life or make yourself miserable with your own irrational thinking.
- No one likes frustration, but we darn well can stand it.
- There are no bad people, just people who at times act badly.
- We do not run the universe; therefore, we cannot get what we want just by demanding it.

The advantages of using the "Let's Get Rational" board game are

1. the game is enjoyable to play, and counseling sessions are attended more regularly,
2. the game format is nonthreatening and encourages even the most resistant clients to "open up,"
3. the forced communication of the squares and cards makes it acceptable for players to share personal information,
4. the game provides a good many "teachable moments," and
5. the game is ambiguous enough that almost any problem can be addressed through the cards and game squares. (Wilde, 1990, p. 4)

Some professionals have spoken of the "horoscope effect," where it seems as though every item (card) is designed specifically for that particular group of players. This phenomenon definitely occurs with LGR.

The game does help reduce depression and helps clients think in a more rational manner (Wilde, 1993b). Forty experimental group subjects played the game one hour a week for seven weeks while forty control group subjects attended their regularly scheduled classes. Dependent measures included the *Children and Adolescent Scale for Irrationality* (CASI); the *Beck Depression Inventory* (BDI), and the *Adjective Generation Technique* (AGT), which is a measure of self-acceptance. Results indicated that subjects who played the game endorsed significantly fewer irrational beliefs than subjects in the control group. Ninth-grade subjects also exhibited more rational thought as measured by the CASI. Tenth-grade experimental subjects were significantly less depressed than tenth grade control group subjects according to scores on the BDI.

Week 5

Homework is not assigned at the end of Week 4 after playing "Let's Get Rational" because students have just had a fun group session, and assigning homework can ruin the upbeat mood. Therefore, there is no homework to go over at the start of Week 5, and the session should begin with "Rate Your Week" or an optional icebreaker activity. Some alternative icebreaker activities are as follows:

- If you could meet anyone who has lived, who would it be and what would you say?
- Without speaking, line up in order from youngest to oldest.
- If you could be any type of animal/vegetable/musical instrument, etc., which would you be?
- What was your most embarrassing moment?
- If you had one wish, what would it be?
- If you were on a desert island and only could have three modern conveniences, which would they be and why?

Lesson for the Week: Self-downing. The objective is to teach students about depression and low self-esteem. It is helpful to go over some of the common warning signs (symptoms) associated with depression which are listed in Chapter 13.

Divide the group in half and ask one of the groups to pretend they are depressed and the other group to act and think normally. Instruct both groups to imagine they have just been rejected for a date by someone whom they really liked. One group is to say the thoughts they have about this event that would cause them to be depressed. The other group is to say thoughts that would indicate disappointment but not depression. Record all responses and analyze them for the presence of the three core beliefs in Beck's cognitive triad: (1) I'm no good, (2) the world is no good, and (3) the future is hopeless.

The depressed group probably will have a lot of irrational self-downing. Ask the group to determine which thoughts from the depressed group are irrational. The entire group the can work together to change the IBs into RBs.

Some questions for discussion are as follows:

1. What does it prove about someone if he/she is rejected?
2. If you are rejected, does that mean you will never be accepted?
3. How can you feel OK about yourself even though you've been rejected?

Homework.   Students are to complete the worksheet called "Reverse the Irrational" (Figure 3). On this worksheet, students practice changing irrational beliefs to rational thoughts.

Week 6

Carry out the "Rate Your Week" exercise, and posttest students using the *Idea Inventory* (Kassinove et al., 1977) to determine if students have learned

---

REVERSE THE IRRATIONAL

Name_____

Directions: For each of the irrational beliefs below, come up with a rational alternative.

1. It is horrible that I have to spend Friday night at home.

2. I hate school, and I shouldn't have to come here.

3. I couldn't stand my friends to know a secret about me.

4. If I make a mistake, it proves how worthless I am.

5. I'll never be able to overcome my past problems.

6. I can't take it when things don't go my way.

Figure 3.   Reverse the Irrational worksheet. Permission is granted to photocopy for classroom use.

the major concepts taught in the group. Now is also an appropriate time to schedule a follow-up meeting in a month to check students' progress.

Lesson for the Week: Dealing with "I-Can't-Stand-It-Itis."   The goal of this lesson is to help students understand how they create anxiety in themselves with their exaggerations about events. Some of the common means of creating anxiety have to do with believing that if a feared event were to occur, it would be so bad a person could not stand it. Another means of producing unnecessary anxiety is by making an event more catastrophic than it is in reality.

Write down the phrase "Taking a *hard test*" and divide the group in half. One half is to think of the kinds of beliefs that would lead to anxiety. The other half is to think of the ideas that would allow a person to remain relatively calm. Analyze the two groups' ideas and determine which were more logical and rational.

If time remains, ask group members to volunteer situations in which they made themselves anxious and try to determine what they were saying to themselves during these episodes of anxiety. Challenge these beliefs with the five questions to determine rationality as proposed Maultsby (1975) that are listed within Week 2 lesson plan.

Wrap-up.   A nice closing activity is to allow each group member to share what he/she has learned in the last six weeks. Next, each student can put his/her name on a piece of paper and have the other group members write something positive about that student. I have used this same activity but instead of passing the paper around, it is pinned to the back of a person's shirt and the comments are written while the paper is hanging from the shirt. Then each member can read to the rest of the group what was written about him/her.

ALTERNATIVE ACTIVITIES

Following is a list of activities than can be substituted or added to any of the lessons.

Hangman

Divide the group in half and have teams take turns deciding if a statement is rational or irrational. If a team answers incorrectly a body part is added to the drawing of a stick person being hung. The first group whose man has all the body parts (head, torso, arms, legs, hands, and feet) is the loser. This same type of activity can be conducted using tic-tac-toe but some students in older grades find tic-tac-toe "uncool."

Self-acceptance Unit (See the self-acceptance sections of Chapter 13 and Chapter 17.)

Human Junkyard (See also "Flat Tire Technique," Chapter 14.)

The idea behind this lesson is that all individuals have both positive and negative qualities. Everybody has some traits that allow them to do certain things very well. Conversely, there are other areas where they are less talented. Students would be foolish to rate themselves as totally worthless simply because they have problems in one or a few areas of their life. The problem areas do not take away from or diminish the positive qualities they possess. I tell the "Human Junkyard" story to illustrate this point.

Pick a student and ask him/her, "If you could have any car in the world, which car would you pick?" When the student answers, give him/her an opportunity to tell a few things about the car and explain why it is such an exceptional automobile. Next ask the student, "If you had this car and it had a flat tire, would you throw the whole car into the junkyard?" When the student says "No," explain that group members are "junking" themselves when they think of themselves as worthless because they have a few problems. Having a problem does not mean that they are worthless; it just means they have an area that needs repair, like a car with a flat tire.

The use of the automobile seems to work exceptionally well with adolescents who seem to have an affinity for cars. An excellent example that might appeal to others was suggested by a former student of mine, Teri Smith. Instead of discussing a car with a flat tire, substitute a great looking outfit that had a missing button. It would be ridiculous to throw out the clothing just because the button was missing, and it is equally nonsensical to "throw out" a complete person because of a minor flaw.

Pie Graph

Another activity designed to get students to stop berating themselves involves the use of a pie graph. Draw a circle and ask a student to tell you what percentage of his/her behavior is "bad." Designate that area of the circle as bad behavior. Next ask what percentage of his/her behavior is "good." If he/she fails to give you two figures that add up to 100%, explain that the rest of the behavior is neutral or neither good nor bad. For someone to be a "bad person," 100% of his/her behavior would have to be bad. That is impossible, since no one can act inappropriately all the time. If a certain student insists that he/she is bad 100% of the time, ask other group members if they ever have witnessed or heard of the individual engaging in any behavior that would not be considered not "bad."

The goal of this activity is to get students to stop thinking of themselves in global terms such as "good" or "bad." Such thoughts are good examples of overgeneralizations that are common in many irrational thoughts. Students can be encouraged to remind themselves that no matter what difficulties they may be having, they are still not "bad." Acting badly is a universal trait that everyone shares from time to time.

Chapter 17

ANGER CONTROL GROUPS

Anger is a significant problem in many students' lives and can cause difficulties for parents, teachers, and society in general. The desire to provide students with skills to manage their anger is increasing. Due to the limited mental health resources available, most schools are choosing to serve students in groups in addition to individual counseling.

If a counselor is considering facilitating an anger control group, a wise procedure would be to sit down with a principal or building administrator and select the students most likely to benefit from the group. Counselors working in an educational setting who have been in a particular building for an extended period of time may already have a good idea of those students who counselors would like to see in such a group.

SIZE OF GROUP

The size of an anger control (AC) group is very important since students in AC groups often have a difficult time behaving appropriately. One might possibly run other groups with 10 to 12 students, but such a large number of students in an AC group is not advisable.

A reasonable number of clients for an anger control group is six in grade school and no more than eight in upper grades. If at all possible, keep the numbers down. As I have stated, when you exceed these numbers you can reach a point of diminishing returns. By wanting to include those two extra students, the integrity of the group is compromised for all.

Managing the behavior of participants in these groups may be even more of a concern than in REBT groups. Please refer back to Chapter 16 to review behavior management techniques to control group members' behavior.

INDIVIDUAL MEETINGS PRIOR TO GROUP (SCREENING)

Just as with REBT groups, each potential group member should be spoken to individually before the group's initial session. The purpose of this screening is to offer the group to the student and assess the student's motivation to change. As has been stated throughout this book, unless students acknowledge that they have a problem, it is difficult to help them. But acknowledgment of a problem is only the first step. Students' also must be willing to change how they look at the world, because the world certainly is not going to change for them. Remember that more students could benefit from such a group than there are slots available. If a student does not appear motivated, move to the next student on the list.

Techniques can be used to raise a student's motivation. Some students view anger as a source of power. As has been discussed, for short periods of time anger can allow individuals to get what they want by intimidating and bullying others. Oftentimes students are immediately reinforced for their anger and do not experience the negative consequences until much later.

Some students will view controlling their anger as a sign that they are "wimps." Try to stress that *anger control is actually a source of power*. Students who let others determine how they feel have less power than students who have control over their emotions and as a result experience the feelings that they chose to experience. When students see the group as being directly beneficial to them, they are more likely to work towards growth rather than disengage.

Try to make the connection between anger and the difficulties that students are experiencing. Many of their problems at school, at home, and with peers are, in all likelihood, at least partially related to their anger difficulties. Help students see the relationship between the detention they received, which is causing them to be grounded for the weekend and have extra duties, and the fact that they lost their tempers. It is not Mr. Clark's fault that the student swore in class; the student swore because he/she got angry.

If a student would like to give the group a try, present a contract for him/her to look over and sign if he/she agrees to the terms. (Refer back to Figure 1 in Chapter 16 for an example.) Emphasize that the student will be expected to live up to the agreements in this contract. If the student does not plan to follow the terms of the contract, he/she should be encouraged not to sign it.

WEEKLY ACTIVITIES

Weeks 1 and 2

The initial two weeks in an AC group are identical to a general REBT group. Refer back to Chapter 16 on REBT groups for this information.

Week 3

After completing "Rate Your Week" and checking on homework, go over the "Where's the Proof?" worksheet (Figure 2, Chapter 16). Spend time disputing why some beliefs are true/rational and some are false/irrational. Help students learn to watch for key words like *must, should, always, never,* etc.

Lesson for the Week: People Make Themselves Angry. During this session is a good time to review the ABCs because most students have not learned them well enough to apply them in problem-solving situations. Students usually can recall that "A" stands for "what happened," "B" stands for "belief" or "thought," and "C" is for a person's "feelings" or "consequences," but they have not learned this to the point of immediate, automatic recall.

During this session (Week 3) is also a good time to review earlier lessons such as "The Blind Man on the Bus" example and the "miracle diet pill" example. If you feel your group has a good grasp of these concepts, proceed as the paragraph below recommends. Some groups will not be ready to move ahead and doing so would prove to be counterproductive. Take your time, and make certain the group has these fundamental concepts down before proceeding.

If the group is ready, use the "Anger Incident Worksheet" (Figure 4). Each member is to complete this worksheet independently. After the group has finished (which usually takes about 8 to 10 minutes), go over the worksheet together so that students can learn from one another's examples.

ANGER INCIDENT WORKSHEET

Name_____
Date_____

Directions: Complete the worksheet with as much accuracy as possible. Pretend you are recording this event as if you were a video camera with sound. A video camera couldn't show someone being mean to you. It could show someone calling you names.

1. When did you make yourself angry? (What date and time was it?)

2. Where were you when you made yourself angry?

3. Who else was present?

4. As specifically as possible, describe what happened.

5. What did you say to yourself to make yourself angry? (Hint: Listen to your self-talk and see if you can hear any *should's, must's,* or *ought to be's.*)

6. How could you change what you said to yourself to change your feelings? (Hint: Try changing your demanding *should's*, etc. to preferences like *I wish . . . , It would be nice . . . , I'd like. . . .*)

Figure 4.   Anger Incident Worksheet. Permission is granted to photocopy for classroom use.

The first four questions are quite simple—questions about the events leading up to students' anger—but many times students will need help with questions 5 and 6. A slight variation that I use with younger groups is to have members complete numbers 1 through 4 independently and then take turns having the group help each member come up with answers to numbers 5 and 6.

When members are ready their answers to question number 5 (What did you say to yourself to make yourself angry?), ask the group to determine whether a belief is rational or irrational. If the belief is irrational (which will be the case in virtually all responses to number 5), why? This is a good chance to assess who is learning to apply these concepts and who is still struggling.

An important part of this lesson is getting students to start listening to their self-talk. This is difficult at first because many students are not aware that they talk to themselves. An incentive to get group members to start listening to their self-talk is to allow them to earn an extra-credit point by writing down five things they say to themselves during the upcoming week. These thoughts do not need to focus on anger. These five thoughts can be any thought, no matter how mundane.

Homework. Students' assignment for the week is to complete an "Anger Incident Worksheet" (Figure 4) using a different situation. Students can choose a situation or event that just occurred or something that happened recently.

Week 4

Complete "Rate Your Week" exercise and review last week's homework. The homework sheets may contain some very interesting items to discuss. The important part of the "Anger Incident Worksheet" has to do with the identification of irrational beliefs and their disputations (numbers 5 and 6). Students are going to have to learn eventually to complete these two important steps independently without the aid of other members.

At this point in the group you will have some students who can find their IBs easily and some that still will be struggling. This is a skill unlike anything they ever have learned before, and with some members it takes time. Be supportive and patient. *Make certain to reinforce attempts to find and dispute IBs even if students were less than perfect in their performance.*

Lesson for the Week: "Let's Get Rational" Board Game. See the section in Chapter 16 that contains information on the use of "Let's Get Rational" (LGR) board game in groups.

Week 5

As was stated in Chapter 16, homework is not assigned the week after playing "Let's Get Rational." Week 5 is started with "Rate Your Week" or an optional icebreaker activity. See the list of alternative icebreakers contained in Chapter 16.

Lesson for the Week: Body Cues. An important step is to have group members learn to identify the physiological cues that are signals of their approaching anger. Each member is given an opportunity to share his/her personal cues; many will be different. Some students will report that they feel warm before they become angry. Some may have reactions such as teeth clenching or fists tightening. Children and adolescents can benefit from paying attention to their cues so that when they feel these changes taking place they can take immediate action to prevent themselves from becoming enraged.

Two techniques that are easy to learn are deep breathing and counting backwards. When clients are aware that they are becoming angry, they can take immediate steps to avoid rage by taking some deep breaths. Slow, deep breaths have a calming effect on the body. Clients also can try saying or thinking a calming word while exhaling. Students can think "relax," "calm down," or "chill out" when they breath out.

Counting backwards from 10 or 20 is also a helpful technique to avoiding anger. It may be a good idea to instruct group members to close their eyes when counting. While these techniques fall under the heading of "distractions," they are still beneficial as they may give students time to think before reacting in an impulsive manner.

Homework.   Have students record one situation each where they might have become angry but were able to remain relatively calm. If a student has no success story to report, he/she can receive credit if it appears as though he/she has been genuinely trying to be successful in other areas of the group and has been participating.

The reason for this homework assignment is to get students to realize that they are able to control their tempers. This also gives the facilitator the opportunity to reinforce students' hard work. A great motivator occurs when students start to realize that they are getting better at handling situations that formerly caused a lot of difficulty in their lives.

Week 6

Complete the "Rate Your Week" exercise and share the group members' success stories. An important point for those in the group who are not being as successful is for them to realize that these skills take time to master. These students have had the habit of making themselves angry for years. They are not going to unlearn these habits completely in a short time.

Week 6 is a good time to posttest students using the "Anger Survey" (Figure 5) to determine if they have learned the major concepts taught in the group.

THE ANGER SURVEY

Name_____
Date_____

Directions: Circle the number that best reflects how strongly you agree or disagree with each statement below.

| Strongly
Disagree | | | | Strongly
Agree |

1. I get angry when things don't go as planned.

    1   2   3   4   5

2. Other people make me angry.

    1   2   3   4   5

3. Life should be fair.

    1   2   3   4   5

4. When I don't do well, I get very angry with myself.

    1   2   3   4   5

5. Things have to be my way or I get angry.

    1   2   3   4   5

6. The world has to be a better place to live.

    1   2   3   4   5

7. My family can make me get angry.

    1   2   3   4   5

8. There are a lot of things that ought to be better than they are right now.

    1   2   3   4   5

9. I can't control my temper.

    1   2   3   4   5

10. I get mad when people don't act like I think they should.

    1   2   3   4   5

TOTAL_____

Figure 5. Anger Survey worksheet. Permission is granted to photocopy for classroom use.

It is also an appropriate time to schedule a follow-up meeting in a month to check their progress.

In Chapter 16 are shown some additional activities that can be substituted for or serve as a supplement to the activities during Weeks 1 through 6.

An additional closing activity is called "The Web." One person starts with a ball of yarn by wrapping the end around his/her finger and passing it to the people in the group who have helped him/her in some manner or with whom he/she "connected" (thus the significance of "The Web"). Whichever group member ends up with the yarn ball goes next by passing the ball to whomever he/she has connected with until everyone has had an opportunity to share. Pretty soon a web of yarn is formed connecting the group to symbolize the ties that have formed in the last few weeks. The yarn can be cut to be worn around members' wrists or kept in a special place as a memento from the group for each member.

If certain students did exceptionally well in group, it might be advisable to have those students serve as advisors or confederates for the next AC group. As is stated in Chapter 16, it is always helpful to have group members who already have exposure to the lessons and ideas in a group to help new members.

ALTERNATIVE ACTIVITIES

Following is a list of activities than can be substituted or added to the curricula.

Hangman

This activity is described in detail in Chapter 16.

Self-acceptance Unit

Many AC clients view themselves as somehow less than adequate and suffer from self-esteem problems. Some group members are in considerable trouble at school and possibly in the community at large. They have been criticized for their behavior or appearance and have come to exist in a state of perpetual anger and/or dysthymia. Viewing themselves as less than adequate only makes overcoming their anger problems more difficult.

Ellis (1977a) pointed out that certain individuals use anger to mask depression and feelings of worthlessness. This is especially true with students in younger grades. Children in early elementary school have a difficult time verbalizing their feelings and tend to express their frustration physically. Be aware that once you get beyond the rage, you may uncover a good deal of depression and feelings of worthlessness.

Human Junkyard (See also "Flat Tire Technique," Chapter 14.)

This activity is described in detail in Chapter 16.

FOLLOW-UP MEETING

The intention of a follow-up meeting is very simple: to assess how students have been doing in managing their anger since the last group meeting. You already may have a pretty good idea of how they have been doing, but a follow-up meeting can be helpful.

In the follow-up meeting, review the ABCs and ask group members to recite the rational belief they use when becoming angry. If students cannot remember their RB, this is a pretty good indicator that they have not been practicing.

A frequently beneficial procedure is to offer students another experience in an AC group if they would like to review the ideas. Anger has been such a part of some students' lives that they feel vulnerable without anger on which to rely to express themselves. In effect, students are making a decision to learn new methods of dealing with the world and the problems life presents. The support students receive from peers during this transformation can be invaluable.

REFERENCES

Beck, A., & Shaw, B. (1977). Cognitive approaches to depression. In A. Ellis & R. Grieger (Eds.), *Handbook of rational-emotive therapy* (pp. 119–134). New York: Springer Press.

Dollard, J., Doob, L., Miller, N., Mowrer, O., & Sears, R. (1939). *Frustration and aggression.* New Haven, CT: Yale University Press.

Dryden, W. (1990). *Dealing with anger problems: Rational emotive therapeutic interventions.* Sarasota, FL: Professional Resource Exchange.

Ellis, A. (1957). Outcome of employing three techniques of psychotherapy. *Journal of Clinical Psychology, 13,* 344–350.

Ellis, A. (1962). *Reason and emotion in psychotherapy.* Secaucus, NJ: Citadel Press.

Ellis, A. (1973). *Humanistic psychotherapy.* New York: McGraw-Hill.

Ellis, A. (1976). The biological basis of human irrationality. *Journal of Individual Psychology, 32,* 145-168.

Ellis, A. (1977a). *Anger—How to live with and without it.* Secaucus, NJ: Citadel Press.

Ellis, A. (1977b). Introduction. In J. Wolfe & E. Brand (Eds.), *Twenty years of rational therapy* (p. 11). New York: Institute for Rational-Emotive Therapy.

Ellis, A. (1985). *Overcoming resistance.* New York: Springer Press.

Ellis, A. (1992). Personal communication, Chicago.

Gibran, K. (1923). *The prophet.* New York: Knopf.

Grieger, R. (1982). Anger problems. In R. Grieger & I.Z. Grieger (Eds.), *Cognition and emotional disturbance* (pp. 46–75). New York: Human Science Press.

Hauck, P. (1980). *Brief counseling with RET.* Philadelphia, PA: Westminster Press.

Kassinove, H., Crisci, R., & Tiegerman, S. (1977). Developmental trends in rational thinking: Implications for school mental health programs. *Journal of Community Psychology, 5,* 266–274.

Lazarus, A. (1978). *In the mind's eye.* New York: Rawson.

Maultsby, M. (1975). *Help yourself to happiness.* New York: Institute for Rational-Emotive Therapy.

McGuire, M. (1990). *Can evolutionary theory help us understand the proximate mechanism and symptom changes characteristic of persons with dysthymic disorder?* A paper presented at the American Psychiatric Association annual meeting, New York, May 14, 1990.

Merskey, H., & Swart, G. (1989). Family background and physical health of adolescents admitted to an inpatient psychiatric unit: 1, principle caregivers. *Canadian Journal of Psychiatry, 34,* 79–83.

Ramsey, R. (1974). Emotional training. *Behavioral Engineering, 1,* 24–26.

Rush, A.J., Beck, A.T., Kovacs, M., & Hollon, S. (1977). Comparative efficacy of cognitive therapy and imipramine in the treatment of depressed outpatients. *Cognitive Therapy and Research, 1,* 17–37.

Trimpey, J. (1992). *The small book.* New York: Delacorte Press.

USA Today. (1992, December 2). Page 1.

Walen, S., DiGiuseppe, R., & Wessler, R. (1980). *A practitioner's guide to rational-emotive therapy.* New York: Oxford University Press.

Wilde, J. (1990). *The let's get rational game.* East Troy, WI: LGR Productions.

Wilde, J. (1992). *Rational counseling with school-aged populations: A practical guide.* Muncie, IN: Accelerated Development.

Wilde, J. (1993a). The problems with self-esteem. *The Journal of Rational Recovery, 5,* 7–8.

Wilde, J. (1993b). *The effects of the let's get rational board game on rational thinking, depression, and self-acceptance in adolescents.* Unpublished doctoral dissertation, Marquette University, Milwaukee, WI.

Young, H. (1974). *A rational counseling primer.* New York: Institute for Rational-Emotive Therapy.

Young, H. (1977). Counseling strategies with working class adolescents. In J. Wolfe & E. Brands (Eds.), *Twenty years of rational therapy* (pp. 187–202). New York: Institute for Rational Living.

Zinker, J. (1978). *Creative process in Gestalt Therapy.* New York: Random House.

INDEX

ABOUT THE AUTHOR

Jerry Wilde is an educational psychologist who works with children and adolescents who have emotional, behavioral, and learning difficulties. Dr. Wilde is also an adjunct faculty member of Ottawa University where he teaches various courses on psychology and psychotherapy. He earned degrees from Luther College and the University of Northern Iowa before receiving a Ph.D. from Marquette University. Other titles by Dr. Wilde include the following:

Rational Counseling with School-aged Populations: A Practical Guide
Rising Above: A Guide to Overcoming Obstacles and Finding Happiness
Anger Management in Schools: Alternatives to Student Violence
Why Kids Struggle in School: A Guide to Overcoming Underachievement

Dr. Wilde's therapeutic board game, *Let's Get Rational*, has been used extensively by counselors around the world. A second board game, *The Use, Abuse, and Recovery Game,* was released in 1993.